Investigating Science with Paper

To Mom and Dad Pickard,
who raised a wonderful daughter

Investigating Science with Paper

by Laurence B. White, Jr.

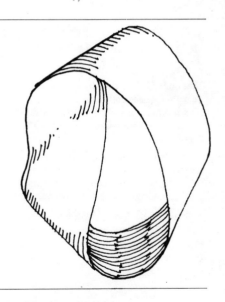

Addison-Wesley Publishing Company

Reading, Massachusetts

Books by Laurence B. White, Jr.
Investigating Science with Coins
Investigating Science with Rubber Bands
Investigating Science with Paper

 An Addisonian Press Book

Text copyright © 1970 by Laurence B. White, Jr.
Text Philippines copyright 1970 by Laurence B. White, Jr.
Illustrations copyright © 1970 by Addison-Wesley Publishing Company, Inc.
Illustrations Philippines copyright 1970 by Addison-Wesley Publishing
Company, Inc.

The Addison-Wesley Publishing Company, Inc.
Library of Congress catalog card number 79-105874
Printed in the United States of America
First printing
SBN: 201-08658-1

Table of Contents

1

Paper Impossibilities

This is your invitation to a science safari! Probably the word safari suggests an excursion into the deepest part of Africa, perhaps in quest of big game animals. But you do not have to go to Africa to have a safari. The word safari comes from the Arabic word *safara*, which simply means a journey, or hunting expedition, and that is exactly what you will be doing in this book. You will have a journey into science, and you will be hunting knowledge and understanding.

Your guide on this safari will be the pages that follow. Your big game will be some pieces of paper, and your trophies will be learning surprising facts and doing surprising things.

In a world filled with computers, space travel, and electronic marvels, you might feel that a piece of paper is much too simple to be considered game for a science safari . . . but you would be very mistaken. Scientific devices, no matter how complex they appear, are based on very simple ideas. Atomic energy, which can generate electricity for entire cities, resulted from scientists studying atoms . . . bits of matter much too small to see. Rockets to the moon are much too complicated for us to build at home, yet you can investigate how they work by simply releasing the nozzle of a blown-up toy balloon. There are many science principles to be studied, and there is a simple way to understand them all . . . just take them one at a time and investigate them. Then they become very simple . . . as simple as a piece of paper!

The investigations you can try with paper will introduce you to many ideas worth thinking about. You will find some that you already know, some that may surprise you, and some that you may not completely understand, but each of them will guide you on a wondrous safari, a journey to help you better understand your world.

WHAT YOU CAN'T DO

This entire book was written about things you *can* do with paper, but, before you begin, just for fun, let's investigate some things you cannot do with paper. You will find there is some good science in studying impossibilities.

Tear a piece of paper (as shown in the illustration on the following page) almost into thirds. Each section should be about three inches wide. The paper should be torn so that there is a tiny bit of paper remaining to be torn between the sections. Now hold each end and try to tear the paper so that the center piece falls out, leaving one piece of paper in each hand and the middle piece on the floor or desk.

Always Two, Never Three

Things Needed:
Piece of paper, about 4″ × 9″

This sounds quite simple, but you will find that you always tear the paper into two parts, never into three! No matter how carefully you try, one piece will always tear off first. To tear the paper into three pieces may not be impossible, but it is so close to it that I'll bet you never succeed! Why? Because to tear both pieces away from the center one at the same time would require all of the following:

1. Both starting tears would have to be exactly the same, with the same amount of paper remaining to be torn.
2. The paper would have to be absolutely the same everywhere. If either place remaining to be torn were thicker or "tougher" than the other, they would not tear the same way.
3. You would have to pull exactly as hard on both sides and at precisely the same time.

4. Both tears would have to move along the paper at the same speed. If either were longer than the other, even by a fraction of an inch, one would beat the other.

Do you understand now why this is practically an impossible investigation? Because so many things must be just so, and are practically never the same twice, this problem is one that is almost impossible to do, even once. Even if you did succeed once, you would probably find it impossible to do again.

Now that you have discovered one thing that you can't do, perhaps you would like to try a few others. Here are three that will get you started:

- How many times can you fold a piece of paper in half? Take a sheet of paper, any size you like, and fold it in half. Then fold the doubled sheet in half again. Continue folding the paper in half. You will find it impossible to fold it in halves *ten* times!

- Cut a strip of newspaper about two inches wide and two feet long. Glue or tape the ends together to make a circular band. Draw a line around the middle of the band and cut along the line with scissors to make two bands. You won't have any trouble doing this. Now make another band, just like the first, but before joining the ends together, *give the paper half a twist*. Try cutting this twisted band into two bands. You'll find it is impossible!

- Take a piece of paper towel. Tear it down, then tear it across. You will find that you can tear quite straight one way, but the tear in the other direction will be crooked and full of zig-zags. It is impossible to tear the towel straight in both directions.

Why are these things impossible? If you really want to know, then you are a real science hunter and you'll find the clues as you travel on your science safari through the pages of this book.

2
Making Paper

Just exactly what is paper? If you have never really thought about it, here are three clues that might help:

The word paper comes from the name of a plant called papyrus. (Paper is used to make books.)

The word book comes from the Anglo-Saxon word *boc* which means "a beech tree." (Books are found in libraries.)

The word library comes from the Latin word *liber* which means "the inner bark of a tree."

From these three clues, you would suspect that paper has something to do with plants and trees. But paper doesn't look much like a plant or a tree, does it? The process of turning plants into paper would certainly appear as a wondrous magic trick to someone who never really took the time to study it. This chapter will give you both the opportunity to understand how this happens, and give you the knowledge you need to make a piece of paper yourself!

If you described paper as "something you can write on," you would only be partly right. In ancient times people scratched words and pictures on pieces of wood or stone; they wrote on leaves, animal skins, or pieces of tree bark. Would you call any of these paper?

The Egyptians pasted dried strips of papyrus plants together and used them to write on. They couldn't fold the sheets, so they rolled them up into scrolls. Were papyrus scrolls paper? Again, it depends on what you call paper, doesn't it?

Perhaps a way to find out what paper is would be to look in a dictionary. The definition would be something like this: "A thin, flexible material in sheets, made from rags, wood pulp, etc., and used to write or print on, wrap, etc." Early man could write or print on all the things he used, but some were not flexible, nor were they made from rags or wood pulp. Paper is really pretty special.

It was an ancient Chinese person who first discovered the secret of papermaking. Nobody knows his name, but it is known that he discovered it around the year 105 A.D., which is over 1800 years ago. What did this Chinese man (or lady) discover? He found that he could take finely shredded fibres from a mulberry bush, cloth, or hemp, soak them in water, spread them on a piece of cloth, dry them in the sun, and produce a flexible sheet of material on which he could write. It might surprise you to learn that the pieces of paper used to make this book were produced in just about the same manner!

Of course, papermaking has improved a great deal since the crude piece of paper our Chinese inventor made, so the paper in this book is much better than his was.   Chemicals and machines can make much finer paper than his, but his basic ideas of using plant fibres, matting in water, and drying, are still the basic steps in papermaking today.

In the past 1800 years papermaking has become a science.   In the early days, papermakers chose fibres from cotton or linen rags as the best materials to work with.   Paper, however, became too important, and as people discovered more uses for it, they demanded more and more.   The need for paper quickly exceeded the amount of rags available.   Someone had to find new materials for papermaking. How?   Out of what?

In the eighteenth century a Frenchman named René Antoine de Réaumur carefully studied a colony of bald-faced hornets.   You may have seen one of their round, football-size, gray paper nests hanging from a tree.   De Réaumur learned that the hornets made the paper for their home by chewing bits of wood and mixing them with saliva.   He suggested that man, too, might make paper out of pieces of wood.

No one paid much attention to de Réaumur's discovery or suggestion for 100 years.   Then, in the nineteenth century, two Germans, Frederic Keller and Henry Volter, remembered his study of the hornets.   After much experimenting, they discovered how to grind wood into the fine fibres required for papermaking.

Since that time man has discovered many tricks for grinding and chemically extracting wood fibres.   But, once you have the fibres, the ancient Chinese method is again used to turn them into paper.

Perhaps the best way to understand this process is to try it yourself. As you perform the investigations that follow, you will be doing the same things our ancient Chinese inventor did 1800 years ago, and a paper company did, not long ago, to make the pages of this book.

FIND THE FIBRES

Paper has been called a "web for words" and that is a very good description. Actually, paper is a mat of tiny plant fibres. These fibres are made of a chemical called *cellulose*. In the plant, these fibres were cemented together with another chemical called *lignin*. By mashing the fibres, and applying certain chemicals, the tiny cellulose fibres were separated. They were then matted together to form a webbing, and a final pressing further flattened the fibres to make a thin smooth sheet.

Seeing the Fibres

Things Needed:
Sheet of newspaper
Hand lens

Tear the sheet of newspaper. Look carefully at the jagged edge of the tear. You will be able to see many tiny cellulose fibres along the edge.

How many fibres are required to make a piece of paper? Certainly it depends on how large the piece of paper is. However, from the above investigation you would probably guess that a fantastic number would be required. You now realize that the fibres are very, very tiny. In fact, it would require about 20 of them, placed end to end, to measure one inch. It would require about 200 of them, placed side by side, to measure the same inch. And here is one of the most surprising figures: Look at just one page of this book . . . it is made of about six million separate bits of fibre!

See How Small the Fibres Are

Things Needed:
Piece of paper towel
Transparent sticky tape

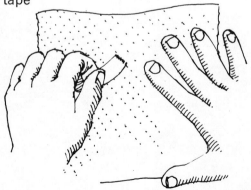

Place the sticky tape down on the paper towel. Press it down onto the paper *very lightly*. Now, gently peel the tape off the paper. Hold the tape up to the light and you should be able to observe the fibres that cling to it.

Although the paper seems to be one solid piece, this investigation proves it is made of many individual fibres. You have simply stripped off some fibres that were close to the surface. This simple method of separating a few fibres allows you to see just how thin and short they actually are.

You might like to try this same investigation by getting and using other kinds of paper. One thing you will want to investigate is if all kinds of paper have fibres that look about the same.

If you would like to save your fibres for later study, you might try sticking the tape down on a piece of black paper. You will find you can observe the fibres right through the tape. They will not only show up well against the black paper, but they will also be permanently preserved!

How can you obtain fibres for making your own piece of paper? You are going to need more than a million of them, so do not be surprised if it takes you a little time to collect them.

Paper can be made from many kinds of plant fibres. Wood is the most common. Straw, bamboo, cornstalks, and other plants have also been used. The finest and most expensive writing papers are made from linen and cotton rags. You should begin your papermaking with one of these.

Fibre Finding—the First Step to Papermaking

Things Needed:
Old cotton or linen handkerchief
Scissors
Small bowl

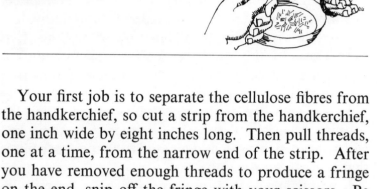

Your first job is to separate the cellulose fibres from the handkerchief, so cut a strip from the handkerchief, one inch wide by eight inches long. Then pull threads, one at a time, from the narrow end of the strip. After you have removed enough threads to produce a fringe on the end, snip off the fringe with your scissors. Be sure to save all the threads, long and short, in the bowl. Continue stripping out individual threads and snipping the fringe until you have separated the entire strip of cloth into tiny threads. This may take as long as an hour, or more. The more patient and thorough you are now, the better your paper will be.

Once you have reduced the cloth strip to tiny threads, your job is not over. These threads are made of many tiny fibres, and it is the individual fibres, not the threads, that you require. Pick up some of the threads in a clump, and snip away at it with your scissors. Continue picking up the threads and snipping until you have reduced the threads to a fine mass of hair-like fibres. Again, the more time you take making the fibres, the more pleased you will be with the final paper.

When you have finally produced a bowl of tiny hair-like fibres of cellulose, you may relax, because turning those fibres into paper is easy from now on.

BLEACH AND BOIL

Naturally, machines are used to separate cellulose fibres in commercial papermaking. These machines could prepare many tons of fibres in the same time it took you to prepare some from your tiny piece of cloth. However, this first step to papermaking is the same whether you are doing it with scissors at home or with giant machines in a factory.

The next important step is *bleaching*. This process will eliminate stains, and soiled fibres will become sparkling clean. This is an important step because any discoloration in the fibres will show on the finished paper.

Science Magic Eliminates Stains

Things Needed:
Piece of paper toweling,
   about 3″ × 6″
Red food coloring
Drinking glass
Laundry liquid bleach

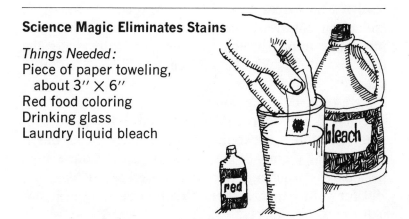

Fill the glass half full of water. Place one drop of red food coloring on the paper strip. Dip the strip into the water and remove it. You will discover that the red color remains on the paper and even stains the water red. Water is not a bleach. If you washed the strip many times in the water, some red color would still remain on it, and the water would remain red also. Now pour a little bleach into the water and slosh it around. (Be careful during this and the following investigation not to spill or splash any bleach on your clothes: it might remove the color. In fact, wearing old clothes is a good idea.) Just like a magician's trick, the red color will mysteriously vanish. When the water turns colorless, dip the paper strip into it. When you remove the strip, you will find that it, too, is completely white again.

How does this trick work? Household bleach is a chemical called *sodium hypochlorite*. Sodium hypochlorite has a very useful chemical in it. It contains a great deal of *oxygen*, a gas, which it releases very easily. Many dyes will join with oxygen to make new, and often colorless, chemicals. Therefore, when you put a dye into a bleach, you do not really make the dye disappear; you simply change it into another chemical you can't see.

Red food coloring joins very readily with oxygen. Green and blue food colorings do not! Try them with your solution. Most inks do disappear; you might try some of them. Some stains, or dyes, require long periods of bleaching. Some require special bleaches. But for your paper, a short bleaching in sodium hypochlorite will do nicely.

Bleaching Your Fibres

Things Needed:
Fibres prepared earlier
Drinking glass
Liquid household bleach
Tea strainer or fork

Place all your fibres in the drinking glass. Pour in bleach until the glass is nearly a quarter filled. Slosh the fibres around in the bleach, making sure that they are all thoroughly soaked. Leave the fibres soaking for about one minute, then carefully pour the bleach down the drain. Either pour the mixture through the tea strainer or hold a fork across the mouth of the glass as you pour, to trap the fibres.

Now fill the glass half full of water, swish the fibres around in it, and carefully drain off the water as you did the bleach. Repeat this several times until most of the bleach has been washed off the fibres.

Finally, after several rinsings, fill the glass with water. You are then ready for the next step—boiling.

Boiling the Fibres

Things Needed:
Glass of water and fibres as described
   in previous investigation
Saucepan
Kitchen range
Spoon, or fork

Pour the water into the saucepan. Be sure all the fibres go in with it. If the fibres are not covered with water, pour in enough water to be sure they are well-covered. Do not be afraid to use plenty of water. Turn on the range, and boil the fibres for 10-15 minutes.

In commercial papermaking, this boiling process is done in huge metal pots called boilers. These turn constantly, preventing the fibres from clumping together. You should stir your mixture with a spoon or fork, occasionally, for the same reason. If you do notice small clumps forming, remove them and mash them between your fingers to separate the fibres before returning them to the pan. Be careful not to burn your fingers.

What is the purpose of boiling the fibres? Later you will stick them together. The finer you make the fibres, the better they will stick. As they boil, the ends of the fibres will fray. The fibres will also swell and become sticky. Both of these actions will be very important in the later steps.

Your fibres are not through with their processing; they are still nothing but fibres. The next step is to mix in *additives;* these are added to the fibres to make them still better for papermaking.

PAPER SOUP

If your paper were being made in a papermaking plant, it would next be moved into a huge vat. Here, three things would happen to it; it would be *diluted, beaten,* and *finished.* To understand these steps, you can do the same things with your fibres.

Two of these steps can be done together; diluting and finishing. Here's how.

Recipe for Paper Soup

Things Needed:
Prepared fibres from previous investigation
Mixing bowl
One-half cup liquid laundry starch
Measuring cup
Spoon
Four cups water

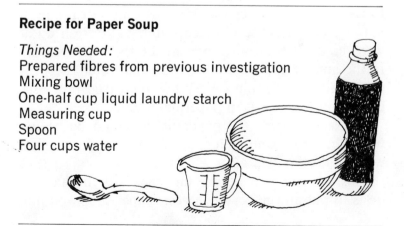

Finishing the paper does not mean what it sounds like. This is not the final step in papermaking. In this case, finishing simply means producing a finish or smooth surface on the paper and making it stiff. Surprisingly, this is done long before the fibres are made into paper. Perhaps your mother finishes your family's shirts or dresses with starch. You will use the same thing.

Pour one-half cup of liquid laundry starch into the mixing bowl. Add four cups of water. Mix them together with the spoon. Pour in the fibres, together with all the water from the saucepan. Stir them about with your spoon. Again, be sure the fibres do not clump together.

In actual papermaking, the fibres are diluted with water to make a paper soup. About one percent of this soup is fibres and ninety-nine percent is water. It is very important to disperse the fibres throughout a large container filled with water. The finer they are dispersed, the better the paper will be. Do not be afraid to use plenty of water for papermaking. Real papermaking machines use so much water that if fresh water were used all the time, soon all of the water supply in the area would be drained. So the water is reprocessed and used again. Very few industrial processes use as much water as in papermaking.

In the huge vat, the paper fibres would be beaten while they were being diluted and finished. You might want to do this step also.

This is a simple papermaking step. All you have to do is to put an egg beater in your paper soup and mix

Beating your Paper

Things Needed:
Paper soup from last investigation
Egg beater
Laundry bluing

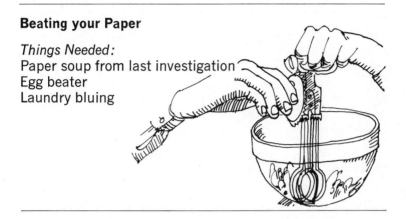

it well. The faster, harder, and longer you beat the mixture, the better your finished paper will be. The beating process will break up the fibres and any little clumps that have formed, and make a smoother soup. More important, however, the beating will further fray the ends of the fibres, and allow them to mat and intermingle better during the final step.

There is one additive you might mix in during this beating process. If your mother has some laundry bluing, add just a few drops to your soup. The bluing will further whiten the fibres and make a cleaner piece of finished paper.

In actual papermaking, other additives might be chalk, glue, or special fibres. These would give special properties to the finished papers. Drop a bit of water on a piece of newspaper and it quickly soaks in. Drop some on a piece of typing paper and it doesn't. Why? The typing paper has an additive, making it water-resistant, which the newspaper doesn't have. Special additives make special papers for special jobs.

GATHERING THE PIECES

If you are becoming a bit discouraged with the length of time it is taking you to make a piece of paper, perhaps it will help to remind you that a real paper-making machine is one of the longest machines used in any factory. Don't give up. You have only three steps left, and each one enables you to see some results of your labor. These final three steps are *screening*, *rolling*, and *drying*.

Netting the Paper

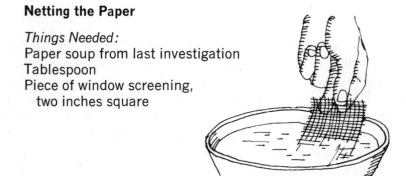

Things Needed:
Paper soup from last investigation
Tablespoon
Piece of window screening,
    two inches square

This is the trickiest, and most important step, so be sure to read the instructions completely before you start. First stir the paper soup thoroughly with your spoon. When the fibres are thoroughly mixed and

suspended in the water, dip the screen into it.   Slide
the screen down to the bottom of the bowl, along
the side, then tip it up and lift.   The fibres will be
trapped on the screen net.   If you have missed some of
the fibres and the paper mat on the screen has some
bare spots, dip it again to net out the remaining fibres.
You should try to produce an even layer of fibres over
all of the screen.   If, on your first try, you simply
make a big clump, just pour the fibres back in, stir
them thoroughly and try again.   When you finally
succeed in obtaining an even layer of fibres, you have
finished with the wet end of your papermaking machine.

Rolling the Mat

Things Needed:
Paper mat on the screen from last investigation
Dry handkerchief
Rolling pin

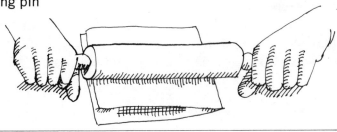

Lay the dry handkerchief flat on a smooth table.
Place the screen and fibre mat on one half of the
handkerchief.   Fold the other half over the mat.   Roll
the rolling pin back and forth over the handkerchief

and mat. You are doing two jobs here: squeezing the water out of the fibres to make it easier to dry and, more important, flattening the fibres into a sheet of paper. As you roll the tiny fibres, the frayed ends are meshing and twining together. The better they lock together, the stronger your paper will be. Continue rolling until the paper appears flat.

Now, very carefully lift the handkerchief off the paper sheet. The paper will probably tend to stick to the cloth, but you will find that you can peel it off carefully. You can be pleased with yourself now, because you are done, and you have really made a piece of paper!

If you tried the "impossible" investigation with the piece of paper in Chapter I, you discovered you could only tear it straight in one direction. In a real paper-making machine the fibres are lined up straight in one direction. You can tear this paper easily if the tear goes with the fibres, but you will make a ragged tear if you go against them. In the paper you make, the fibres will not be lined in one direction, so your paper tears equally well in all directions.

Now you have one final, and obvious, step left:

Drying the Paper

Things Needed:
Paper from above investigation,
   on its wire screen

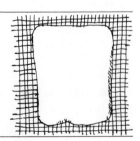

Set the screen aside until the paper is thoroughly dry. This will probably mean leaving it overnight. When it is dry you may pick the paper off the screen, trim the ends and sides to make it square and—and this is the big moment—try writing on it.

What should you write? How about—A PIECE OF 100% RAG PAPER MADE BY (YOUR NAME)? After all, that's what it is, and you really did make it!

SPECIAL PAPERS

Each kind of paper is made to do a special job. Newspaper does not have to be smooth or last very long. Newspaper is made of 100% wood. The typing paper used in writing this book had 25% cotton fibre content. You can also find wrapping papers, cardboard, tissue paper, tracing paper, carbon paper, and thousands of others. What makes each one special? Perhaps it's the additives that went into them, or perhaps they were made in a special way.

Newspaper and typing paper are made of different materials. Here is an example of a paper that is "different" because of what was added to it:

The Special Paper of a Dollar Bill

Things Needed:
Dollar bill
Bright light

Lay the dollar bill in the palm of your hand and look at it. It appears to be an ordinary piece of paper. Imagine how easy it would be to copy or *counterfeit* a dollar bill if it were just a plain piece of paper with fancy designs on it. The government, however, prints dollar bills on paper made especially for dollar bills. No papermaker can make paper like this unless the government orders him to. If you made paper like this, you would be breaking the law.

What makes this paper special? Hold the dollar bill between a bright light and your eyes so that you can look through the paper. If you look carefully you will see that some tiny threads in the paper are dark colored. Perhaps you will see that some are red and some are blue. Most of them are white, so the bill looks white, but just enough red and blue fibre threads are added to make this paper different from any other paper made in the United States. And what about five, ten, twenty, or larger denomination bills? Are they also printed on this special paper?

Paper can also be different because of the way it is processed. Paper with a very smooth surface has been pressed through very powerful rollers. Some tissues are scraped across a knife edge to give them a ruffled finish. Transparent papers result from fibres that are ground very finely.

One interesting process you can investigate is called watermarking. It is generally used on fine papers that the manufacturer is proud of. It is a way of putting an invisible mark on a piece of paper that doesn't interfere with the printing.

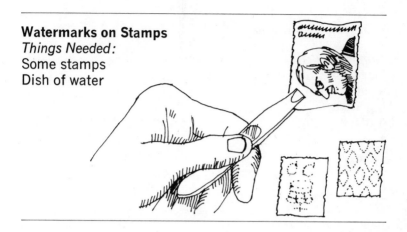

Watermarks on Stamps
Things Needed:
Some stamps
Dish of water

Many stamps are made special by laying the wet paper on wire meshes with certain designs and rolling them. The design is embossed into the paper. Once the paper dries, the embossed design becomes almost invisible. If you have several stamps, perhaps you can find one with a watermark (not all stamps have them). Simply soak the stamp in a dish of water for a few minutes. When it is thoroughly wet, hold it up to the light, back side toward you. If it has a watermark, you will be able to see the design easily. If the stamps have glue on the back do not soak them in water. Stamp collectors use a detecting fluid available at a hobby shop, which shows the watermark but does not dissolve the glue.

Rather than search for watermarks on stamps, you might enjoy making your own watermarks on the piece of paper you have made, or any piece of writing paper. Here's how:

Your Own Watermark

Things Needed:
Two sheets of paper
A window pane
A pencil
A pan of water

Dip one sheet of paper in water for about ten seconds. Stick this wet sheet against the window pane. Lay the dry sheet of paper on top of it. Without moving either of the sheets, write or draw a design on the dry sheet of paper. Be sure to press down hard with the pencil so that the impression of your writing is transferred to the wet sheet. Remove the dry sheet and peel the wet one off the window. Put the wet watermarked sheet aside to dry. While it is wet you will be able to see your writing clearly, but once it dries, the writing will become invisible.

Although you will not be able to see your watermark easily once the paper dries, you can bring it back any time you like simply by dipping it in water.

Dip sheets of different kinds of writing or typewriter paper in water to see if they have watermarks. Can you see them in the dry paper if you hold the paper up to a light?

You can write an invisible message to a friend using watermarks, and it might be a "scientific" way of inviting people to a party.

There are many special papers in your house and school. It might be fun to try to make a collection of as many as you can find. Perhaps you might try to guess what made them special. Was it what they were made from, what was added to them, or how they were processed?

Remember though, no matter how special a piece of paper may be, its most important job is being a web for words. We would never know what ancient peoples learned, or what is happening in the world today, or whether our homework is right or wrong, if it were not for this important invention. Paper also enables us to tell other people what we know. Where would this book be without it?

3

Absorbing Paper

The next time you have a soft drink and use a paper-covered straw, try this: Place one end of the straw on the table and slide the paper covering down so that it crumples around the bottom of the straw like an accordian. Next, place the crumpled paper bundle on a saucer and drip a little water on it, using the straw as your "medicine dropper." Watch the paper. It will begin to wriggle, wave about, and grow longer. Probably it will remind you of a snake or a caterpillar.

This, you will find, is an "absorbing" trick. You will be absorbed in watching the gyrations of the paper snake and, of course, the trick works because the paper absorbs the water.

Everyone knows that paper gets soggy when it is wet, but, as a science investigator, you ought to ask *why*, or *how*. Perhaps you can learn more about what happens when paper and water meet.

MAKING WATER CLIMB A HILL

Rivers flow downhill into the ponds and oceans. Waterfalls always fall down. The water from a faucet falls down into the sink. If I were to ask you which way water moves, you would undoubtedly answer down, and yet, all around you there are examples of water moving up. Can you think of one?

If you have difficulty thinking of an example, it may be because you do not actually see the water moving; you just know that it must be doing so. How about in a tree? A tree, like most plants, relies on its roots to obtain water from the soil. This water must then move up and flow to every living part of the tree. You know that it must flow up, but just how does it do it?

Actually, this mystery has interested many scientists for many years ... and they still do not completely understand it. Probably water moves up inside a tall tree by several different processes working together. Some of these processes are very complicated, but some are quite simple. You can investigate one of the simple ones with a piece of paper toweling.

A Water Ladder

Things Needed:
Drinking glass ¼ filled with water
Strip of paper towel, 6″ × ½″

Fold over an inch of paper on one end of the strip. Hang the strip over the rim of the glass so that the paper touches the water. Observe what happens. You will notice the water beginning to creep up the strip. If you wait long enough, the water will creep right over the rim of the glass and may even drip onto the tabletop.

This strange creeping of water uphill is called *capillary action*. One way water moves up tall trees is by capillary action. How does it work?

First, you must not think of a sheet of paper as a solid object. Remember that it is actually a web made of tiny fibres pressed close to one another. Between the fibres are spaces that can fill up with water.

Second, you must look carefully at a glass of water. At first glance the surface of the water appears flat, like a tabletop . . . but this is not true. If you look at the same surface from the side, you will agree that it actually curves up at the edges where it touches the glass sides. Dip a pencil into the water and you will observe the water curving up a bit where it touches the pencil. The center of the water surface, which is not touching anything, is actually lower than the edges.

In your investigation, when the paper towel strip touches the water, the water runs into the spaces between the fibres. Like the glass or the pencil, every fibre that touches the water causes the water to curve up around it. When the edges of the water surface curve, and pull upward, they tend to pull the rest of the water upward also. In a glass of water the center is much too wide and heavy to move up, so it falls back. Finally a balance is reached between the edges moving up and the center pulling them back down. This results in the curved surface you observed. But suppose the center were very small and not very heavy? Don't you suppose that the edges would then be able to lift it up? This is exactly what happens between the fibres in the paper towel strip.

Water is attracted by solid objects, like the glass, pencil, and paper fibres. If the spaces in the solid objects are small enough, this attraction will cause the water to move toward, and up into the spaces. This, then, is capillary action.

If you put a thick steel knife or piece of glass in water, the water would not creep up inside of it. There are no spaces small enough for water to fit between. The spaces are important and necessary. Their size and shape will make capillary action work better or less well. To prove this, you might ask: "Is there any difference between different kinds of paper?".

A Capillary Contest

Things Needed:
Drinking glass ¼ filled with water
Food coloring (any color)
Strips of paper, 6″ × ½″:
  Paper towel, Cardboard,
  Blotting paper, Toilet paper,
  Facial tissue, . . . or any others
  you might have available

Fold each strip an inch from one end. Hang the strips as in the last investigation, over the edge of the quarter-filled glass of water into which a drop of food coloring has been stirred. Watch as the water creeps up each strip. On which strip does the water climb quickest? Which one will let it climb over the rim of the glass? Perhaps you might try to guess before you actually begin this investigation. Capillary action works best in the papers with the most, best shaped, and, often, longest spaces in them. Very often the kind of paper that is the best to write on is the poorest for capillary action. Can you explain why this might be so? If not, you can find the answer in the chapter on paper making.

ABSORBING THE SCIENTIFIC METHOD

Do you know how a scientist solves problems? How does he discover things that have never been known before? It is not really as impossible as it sounds. A scientist uses the *scientific method* to study the problem. All he does is take his problem step by step. Here's how:

First he finds a puzzle that he doesn't understand—perhaps one that nobody has ever understood. Then he does the following . . . one after another:

1. He makes a guess at *why* it happens. This is called an *hypothesis*, which is just a fancy way of saying "a guess."
2. Next, he *experiments*, to see what actually happens.
3. As he experiments, he very carefully *observes* and *studies* what is happening.

4. Last, he makes a *theory*, which is his explanation of the actual cause of the happening. This may be the same as his hypothesis, or it may be very different because of what he observed during his experiment.

Here is an investigation that will give you a chance to use the scientific method. Please read the instructions *before* you begin.

The Great Paper Race

Things Needed:
Soup bowl ½ filled with water
Sheet of paper toweling cut
as shown in illustration
(*Size of strips is not important,
but make one wide, one thin*)

Now, before you begin, here is what you are going to do: You are going to lower the paper strips into the water so that the two free ends touch at the same time. Naturally, once the strips touch the water it will start to creep upward. Here is the problem you must solve using the scientific method:

In which strip, the thin or the wide, will the water creep up the faster?

Can you solve this problem using the scientific method? Here are the steps you must take:

First make a guess (hypothesis) as to which strip will win the race. To make this guess you should use everything you really know, or think.

Second, lower the ends of the paper strips into the water. This is your experiment. Hold the papers level with the bowl, and hold them steady with just the ends touching.

Third, watch what happens very carefully. Even if you guessed wrong, remember . . . and believe . . . what you observe. If you really doubt your results, cut another paper and try it again. Scientists often try the same experiment dozens of times to be sure of the results.

Fourth, even if you did guess wrong, you must *explain* why that particular strip won the race. If you guessed wrong, but can now explain why you were wrong, you are still being a good scientist. A scientist's job is not to be 100% right on all his guesses. His job is to conduct experiments and attempt to explain what he sees. Your explanation, right or wrong, is now your *theory*.

Once the scientist has a theory, he would probably tell it to other scientists to see whether they agree with him. If they don't, they might suggest other ideas. These other ideas would be their hypotheses and our scientist might think of other experiments to see whether his theory or his friend's guesses were correct. Just like the scientist, you might like to check your theory on the Great Paper Race with your friends or teachers to see whether or not they have other ideas.

Remember that the scientific method is used not only by scientists; it works for most other people too.

Suppose you liked playing baseball but you couldn't hit the ball well. You might first guess what is wrong, experiment the next time your team practices, make a theory that you are "swinging the bat too soon," and then tell the coach your theory. Haven't you actually used the scientific method? Even if your coach has other ideas, if you continue to think this way the chances are very good that you will be hitting the ball very hard, very soon!

Girls also use the scientific method. Suppose you weren't having any luck at all trying to bake a cake. Every time you tried the cake fell as flat as a pancake. Perhaps in reading the cookbook you learned that baking powder was an important ingredient in cake-making. You might make a guess that you were not using enough baking powder. You have just made a hypothesis! Next, you might try baking a cake using more baking powder than before. You have just made an experiment! You might see that, this time, the cake rose beautifully. You have just made an observation! Then you might decide that, from now on, you should use more baking powder if you are going to always make perfect cakes. You have just made a theory! If all of your later cakes turn out perfectly you will know that your theory is correct, and this is the one final step in the scientific method . . . proving that your theory works every time.

So, you see, the scientific method is not at all as mysterious as it first appears. It is used by everyone. You and I use it practically every day. We call it applying our "common sense."

CHROMATOGRAPHY

Now that you have learned that water can move upward through a piece of paper by capillary action, if you are like many people, you might be saying, "So what?". Some people do not seem to think anything is worth knowing unless there is some practical use for it. Some scientists, however, study things which seem to have no use at all. This kind of study is called pure research. Why do they do it? Why should you?

Once some pure-research scientists studied atoms. Atoms were too small, too unknown, and too unimportant to be worth studying. Today we are using atomic energy to make electricity, turn powerful motors, and cure many diseases. If no scientist had studied atoms nobody would have ever known how very useful they could be. Scientists do pure research simply to understand our world better; frequently someone discovers a use for what they learn. You, too, should never hesitate to study what may seem to be unimportant things if they interest you. The people who study such things are often the same people who make the most important discoveries.

What use could we find for the way water moves through a piece of paper? Surprisingly, one very important use has already been discovered, and you can experiment with it. This subject is called *paper chromatography*. From its name you already know that it has something to do with paper, and its last name, chromatography, means *color* (chroma) and *write* (graphein).   Put them together and it means "to write with colors on paper".   Here is one way you can introduce yourself to color-writing:

Roll the end of the paper strip around the center of the pencil and fasten it in place with the paper clip. Place a drop or two of the green food coloring in the center of the strip.   The illustration will help you do this properly.

Strip Chromatography

Things Needed:
Strip of paper towel, 6″ × 1″
Drinking glass
Green food coloring
Rubbing alcohol
Pencil
Paper clip

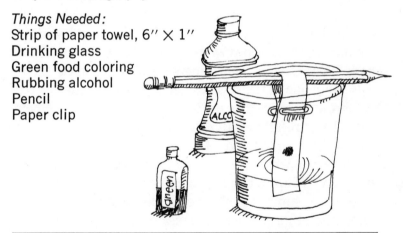

Fill the drinking glass one-quarter full of rubbing alcohol.   Lay the pencil across the mouth of the glass so that the lower end of the paper strip is touching the alcohol.   Now, put the investigation aside for several hours.

When you return, the alcohol will have crept up the paper strip past the spot of food color. The various chemicals making up the food coloring will have been absorbed by the alcohol and dragged along with it. Most surprisingly, you may discover several different colors making up the smudge you have produced.

Where did the colors come from? Do you suppose that the different chemicals making up the green food coloring might have been different colors, and that they were somehow separated from one another by the alcohol? Well, this is exactly what happened! The different chemicals were absorbed by the alcohol in different amounts. Some were absorbed easily and were carried higher, while others did not mix readily with the alcohol and traveled upward only a short distance. You have succeeded in separating several well-mixed chemicals using one of the simplest techniques ever discovered!

Chromatography is an important test for the scientist. By carefully analyzing the chemicals making the colors, he is able to identify them. In this way he can easily learn what the original solution was made of. It's easy to appreciate that paper chromatography is a science subject well worth knowing about and, remember, that it works because of that "unimportant" idea of capillary action and how water moves through paper.

You might say, "But I don't use water in this investigation, I use alcohol." Can you guess why? Alcohol moves through paper by capillary action much the same as water. However, alcohol dissolves things differently. Does this give you a clue? If not, try this:

Water Chromatography

Things Needed:
Some materials as in
    last investigation
Water instead of alcohol

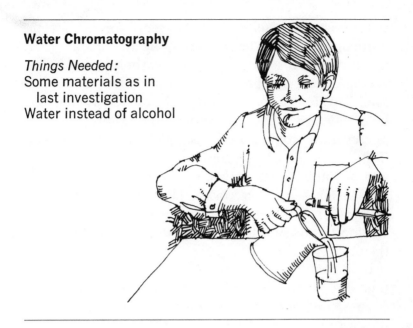

Use the same materials, in the same manner, as you did in the last investigation, Strip Chromatography, except use one-quarter glassful of water instead of alcohol. Do you get blotches of different colors as you did with the alcohol? No, because the food color chemicals mix readily with water, so they will all be carried evenly along with the water. This results in a plain green smear. The top of the smear will be made of the same chemicals as the bottom.

Do not be disappointed that this investigation with water chromatography does not work well. It reminds us that the solution used to carry the chemicals (chemists call this the *solvent*) is extremely important. Often a scientist must select just the right solvent for the particular material he is attempting to separate. He might choose a solvent like ether, carbon tetrachloride, acetone, benzene or carbon disulphide. He might even find that paper does not work as well as charcoal, lime, talc, or sugar to "write" the colors on. No matter how complicated his combination might be, it still depends on the simple idea of capillary action and, if you understand this, you will always understand how this investigation works. This reminds us that it is usually fun to know the basic ideas in science, even if we don't know what good they are when we first learn them.

If you would like to experiment further with chromatography, there are several different ways it can be done. A method which produces pretty rings of color uses a round piece of paper. Here's how:

Circle Chromatography

Things Needed:
Sheet of paper toweling
Green food coloring
Rubbing alcohol
Scissors
Small soup bowl

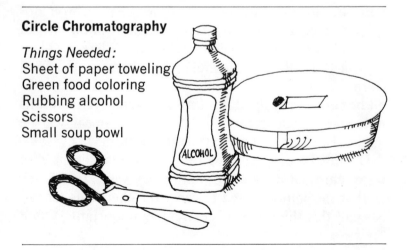

Cut a circle out of the paper towel a bit bigger than the top of the soup bowl. Cut a flap in the center of the disc, making sure that it is long enough to fold down and touch the bottom of the bowl when the disc is resting on top, like a lid. (See the illustration.) Place two drops of green food coloring at the fold of the flap. Pour about half an inch of alcohol into the soup bowl and place the disc on top. Fold the flap down so that it dips into the alcohol. Leave the investigation set up like this, undisturbed, for about two hours. When you return you should find rings of color on the paper disc.

If you would like to learn more about the fascinating science of chromatography, you can find information about it in chemistry books at your local library. If you would prefer to discover other things by yourself, here are some investigations you might start with:

- Try different food colors. Are they made of different chemicals?

- Mix two, or more, food colors together. Can you separate them?

- Try water chromatography with a spot of ink from a ball pen.

- Plants are green because they contain *chlorophyll*, a green chemical. Cut up some leaves and soak them in a covered dish containing a little alcohol. (Spinach leaves work well.) In a few days, when the alcohol turns green, use this solution in the glass. As the alcohol and chlorophyll creep up a paper strip various other chemicals may separate out. Can you find *carotene* (orange) and *xanthophyll* (red)? These give the autumn leaves their colors.

- Do different kinds of paper work better than paper towels? Do they work faster or slower?

- Your father might have some denatured alcohol, or perhaps some acetone in his shop. Try these or other solvents instead of rubbing alcohol. (Note: do not breathe these solvents.)

As you try the above investigations, plus any others you can think of yourself, it is easy to imagine the thousands of similar experiments that scientists have tried in order to learn what they know about chromatography. Every experiment they tried was a mystery when they began, just as your investigations are. They did not know what would happen or whether it would be useful later on. This is pure research. Pure research is important in many ways, and it is also one of the most rewarding parts of science, because whether or not an experiment works out the way a scientist expected, he always learns something from it. This is the only part of science where an experiment never fails!

WATER THROUGH PAPER

You are already well aware of the fact that paper is a web of plant fibres which water can "fit between." Some chemicals, however, are not able to fit into these spaces simply because they are too big. This easy-sounding idea is very important to the scientist. He uses this fact to help him *filter* solutions.

To understand how this works, suppose we had accidentally mixed together some salt and some small stones. How could we separate the salt from the stones? Wouldn't you agree that the easiest method might be to sift the mixture through a piece of window screening? Only the tiny salt grains would fit through the openings, and the stones would remain trapped on top. If the screening had smaller openings it could be used to separate still smaller objects. A piece of paper can be considered just that . . . a screening with very, very tiny openings. Because of this, a scientist frequently uses *filter paper* in many experiments. You might enjoy investigating how he does it.

How to Fold a Filter

Things Needed:
Small kitchen funnel
Piece of paper towel about 5″ square
Drinking glass

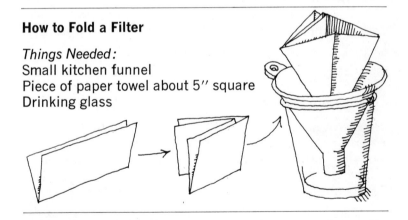

Place the funnel in the glass. Fold the square of paper in half, then in half again. Open one side of the paper square so that it will fit into the funnel. Place the paper into the funnel in the glass. You will notice if you now poured water into the funnel it would be trapped inside the paper, and it would have to seep through the paper in order to drip into the glass.

If you ever see a piece of filter paper in a chemistry laboratory it will not look like yours. Most filter paper is round. Try cutting a circle out of a sheet of paper toweling. (You can draw around a saucer.) The round paper is folded in the same manner: in half, then in half again. You will find that a round sheet is actually easier to use than a square one, but for the investigations that follow, you may use whichever shape you prefer.

Sprinkle pepper into the water until the surface is well covered. Stir the mixture until you can see the tiny pepper grains scattered throughout the water. Now, carefully pour the mixture into your filter, making sure that all of it goes into the paper and

---

Filtering the Pepper

Things Needed:
Filter funnel from last investigation
Drinking glass ¼ full of water
Pepper shaker
Teaspoon

none runs down the side or along the funnel beside the paper.

When all of the water has dripped into the glass, look inside the filter paper. You will discover that most of the pepper has been caught by the paper screen simply because it couldn't fit through the tiny openings. You may remove the paper, and the pepper, and throw it away.

Did your filter remove all of the pepper from the water? The chances are, it didn't! You can prove this to yourself by looking through the water toward a light. It will probably have a slight brownish color.

Why didn't your filter remove all of the pepper? Naturally, because some of the tiniest pepper grains were small enough to slip through the spaces in the paper. Can you think of a way to make a filter work even better?

Find a Finer Filter

Things Needed:
Same equipment as used in last investigation
Paper toweling
Newspaper

 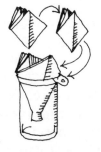 

1   2   3

To build a better filter you might use any one of three different methods. You can try each one yourself to discover which method works best for you.

Method I: Refiltering

Filter the water and pepper mixture as before, through a paper towel filter. Throw away the paper and make a new paper towel filter. Pour the once-filtered solution through the new filter, then throw this filter away. If you can still detect the pepper in the water, repeat the process with still another filter. How many times must you refilter the solution before you finally "catch" all of the pepper? (Or, can you ever get rid of it all?)

Method II: Multiple Filtering

Make a filter out of paper toweling and place it inside the funnel. Then make another one and place it inside the first one. Pour a pepper and water solution through both filters. Do you suppose the second filter will catch the pepper that the first one misses? If the solution is still not clear with two filters, perhaps you could make a funnel that contained three, or more, filter papers.

Method III: Finer Filter

You now know that the biggest problem with the paper towel filter is simply that the holes are too big. Perhaps a paper with smaller holes would do a better job. Does a newspaper have smaller spaces between the fibres? Try using a piece of newspaper as a filter to separate the pepper from the water. A filter paper used in a chemistry laboratory has very tiny holes. It is a very special piece of paper.

You will find that the smaller the holes the longer it will take for the water to drip through it. In fact, you can more or less determine how small the holes are by observing how long it takes for the water to pass through. Perhaps you can find a paper with even smaller holes than newspaper or paper toweling.

A scientist might use any one of these methods to separate materials from mixtures. Frequently he uses combinations of them. He might use several sheets of very fine paper (multiple filtering through a fine filter), and he might even do it several times (refiltering) before he is satisfied.

Remember too, that in our investigations we have been trying to get back the clear water that we started with. Often the scientist uses filtering for just the opposite purpose. If we had accidentally spilled our pepper into the water, and we wanted to get our pepper back again, this would still be the right way to do it. If the scientist wished to separate a non-dissolving chemical mixed with water he certainly would use a filter, save the chemical caught by the paper, and throw the water away.

FORTUNE TELLING FISH

Would you like to finish this chapter with a bit of fun? Here is a wonderful toy that depends on the exact things you have been reading about. It is surprising how much science we can discover in toys. Often the simplest science principle can appear quite miraculous to someone not familiar with it. Such is the case of the "Fortune Telling Fish."

The Fortune Telling Fish probably originated in Japan. No one knows just how long ago, probably as long ago as the invention of *cellophane*. Cellophane is a kind of transparent paper made from the cellulose in plant fibres. You have probably seen it as candy or cigarette package wrapping. You will require a piece of cellophane for this investigation, so you should learn to recognize it. Do not mistake it for synthetic clear plastic. Cellophane looks somewhat the same, but most plastics are stretchy and do not crease easily. Cellophane, on the other hand, is stiff, creases easily, and makes a crackling noise when it is crushed. Most plastics refuse to absorb any water, but cellophane will absorb a little bit. Because of this difference a Fortune Telling Fish has to be made of cellophane.

If you would like a Fortune Telling Fish, they are often available in novelty stores for a few cents. But, better still, perhaps you would like to make your own.

Make a Fortune Telling Fish

Things Needed:
A very *thin* piece of cellophane, ¾″ × 2″
Scissors

Trace the design of the fish on the cellophane, using the illustration as a pattern. Your fish does not have to look exactly like this one, but the size is rather important.

This cellophane fish is very *hygroscopic*. This big word should remind you that we are investigating science as well as fun. "Hygro" means water, and "scopic" means to view or find. Hygroscopic then means to find water. The cellophane will readily absorb water wherever it can. The fish you have made, besides being a toy, is a very sensitive moisture detector.

You are probably wondering how to use your fish to tell fortunes. Actually it is not able to tell your fortune at all, but here is how to use it: place the fish on the palm of your hand and watch it for a minute or two. The fish will suddenly "come to life." It will wiggle and curl up in a most mysterious manner.

If you had bought your fish at a novelty store you would also receive instructions for determining your future from the way it curls. The fortunes differ, depending on which company made that particular fish. Here is one formula you might follow:

Head moves ...... You'll be good

Tail Moves .... You'll be bad

Head and Tail Move You'll be good and bad

Sides curl .... You'll marry your sweetheart

Turns over .... Your sweetheart will marry
                       her sweetheart

Doesn't move ..... You're dead

Curls into circle ... Wow!

Actually, I could have written any future for you. This is really a silly method for telling the future. No scientist really believes there is any way to do that. However, you can have fun by making up fortunes of your own for the fish.

What's really happening here? The simple truth is that you, and any friend you might try it on, *perspire*. A great deal of the water we drink is eliminated through our skins in the form of perspiration, or sweat. On a hot day, or after hard exercise, we are very much aware of our perspiration; however, this is a process that goes on all the time . . . night and day . . . through all parts of our skin. Generally we are not aware of this water on our skin, but if we place a device sensitive to moisture on the skin we can prove that the water is there. Your fish is just this sort of device.

When the fish is placed on your palm the moisture from perspiration flows into the tiny spaces in the cellophane by capillary action. The water causes the spaces to swell and, in effect, the fish becomes larger. The bottom of the fish swells first and bends away from the dry upper part. The fish curls up. Those parts of the fish touching your palm will receive the most moisture, so they swell and curl up first. Rather than telling your fortune, this fish is actually telling you that you are perspiring and it is showing you which parts of it are touching you and which parts are not.

This chapter began with an investigation which produced a moving paper "snake". Can you see how the snake and the fish have a great deal in common?

I hope that you are not too disappointed to learn that your Fortune Telling Fish can't tell fortunes at all.   It really serves as a reminder that many of the seemingly unexplainable occurrences you might hear or read about can often be easily explained with simple science if one takes the time to thoroughly investigate them.   It's very possible that ghosts, Unidentified Flying Objects, sea serpents, and the like, might some day be found to be caused by science facts that no one had really investigated before.

4

Paper Engineering

Would you like to build a skyscraper? How about a giant bridge? If you think this kind of work would be exciting and fun, you might like to be an engineer. An engineer works with science, too. He has studied many of the rules of science and he applies these rules and makes things which use them.

Someone once said that a scientist discovers an idea and an engineer discovers what to do with it. There are many different kinds of engineers. Some make motors, delicate instruments, rocket ships, or submarines. Some devise special lights, radios, power plants and toys. In fact, just about anything you can think of that is man-made probably involved some kind of engineer.

THINKING LIKE AN ENGINEER

An engineer who builds a building has a complicated job. He must think about what kinds of materials he will use, how to fasten them together, how people will move about in the building, and even what the land under the building is like. He must think about every part of the building and its surroundings. To start with, let's think about the materials. Rather than steel and wood, however, we can use paper to understand how an engineer thinks.

A piece of writing paper is not very strong. It is floppy and easily folded.

Have you ever seen a piece of corrugated cardboard? It is often used to make shipping boxes. Some corrugated boxes are strong enough to hold you up if you stand on them. Corrugated cardboard is made of paper, but it is strong paper. It was invented by an engineer who wondered how paper could be made stiffer. Engineers can make building materials stronger in this same way.

Can you think like an engineer? Here is a puzzle to solve right now. Try to do it before you read the next section.

Balance a Paper on its Edge

Things Needed:
Sheet of typing paper, 8½" × 11"

Place one edge of the sheet on the table. Let the paper go. It falls over. You cannot make the paper balance on its edge this way. There are, however, many things you might do to the paper to help it balance on one edge. One is very simple . . . just crease it down the middle! If you open it out to a V shape, it is easy to set it upright on the table. How many other ways can you think of to help it balance? You'll get many ideas from the investigations that follow.

MAKING PAPER STRONGER

I'll bet you would think that a bar of steel ten feet long, six inches wide, and half an inch thick would be very strong, wouldn't you? You certainly couldn't bend it or tie it into a knot!

Suppose that same bar were part of a skyscraper. It might have to support many tons of bricks, or perhaps a floor with people walking on it. Would the bar be strong enough to support several tons of weight? Probably not. An engineer would consider a flat bar of steel very, very weak. He would have to devise some method of making it stronger.

To appreciate his problem and discover a solution, you might try this investigation with a sheet of newspaper.

Just how "strong" is a sheet of newspaper? Open a full sheet of newspaper paper out to its full width. Hold the paper by one corner and place the *diagonal* corner on the palm of your other hand. Can you balance the paper by one corner?

Balance a Paper

Things Needed:
A full (two page) sheet
of newspaper

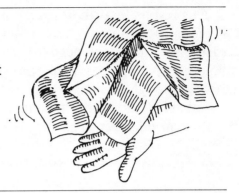

Before you look at the solution, try to devise a method by yourself. This is just the kind of problem an engineer might have to solve.

The problem is, as you've already discovered, that the paper is not even strong enough to support its own weight. It is floppy and keeps folding over in the middle. Suppose there were some kind of support on the side that held the paper up and prevented it from falling over. Would this help?

You can make such a support out of the paper itself. This is a standard trick used by engineers. To do it, simply crease the paper down the center of the diagonal, then fold the sides back. (See illustration.)

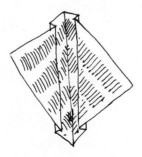

This results in a rib down the middle. Try balancing it on your palm now. You will find that you can do it easily. If the paper bends to either side, the rib will hold it up. This simple trick has made the paper strong enough to support its own weight, which is an impossible feat without the crease.

Can an engineer crease a piece of steel in the same way? You'll find that he can, and does do it in many different ways, in the next section.

DESTRUCTIVE TESTING

We have learned that simply by folding a sheet of paper, it will support its own weight. There are many other ways you could crease the sheet, more complicated than just a V fold. If your problem were to simply balance a sheet of paper on one edge, you should be able to solve it by folding and creasing the paper in many different ways. Let's make the problem a bit more difficult. Can you make the paper support something besides its own weight?

A Book on Paper

Things Needed:
Several 8½″ × 11″ sheets of paper
A book (this one will do nicely)

Fold a sheet of paper in a V shape and stand it on edge on the table. Place the book on top. Will it support the weight of this book? No. The paper can hold itself up but crumples when more weight is added. Can you fold one of the other sheets in another way which will support the book? The illustration shows several ways I discovered to do it.

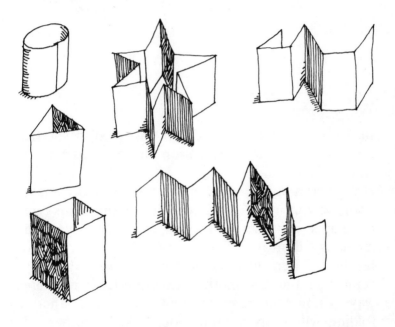

Once you have folded several sheets into shapes that will support the book, there is still one other investigation you should make. Do you suppose that all of the folded sheets are equally strong?

Once an engineer devised a method for making flat materials stronger by folding, he would test them to determine whether his particular method was better

Squashing Papers

Things Needed:
Papers from last investigation
Several books, all the same size

than others. One way of doing this is called "destructive testing." The investigation above shows how this can be done.

Support a book on each of the papers. Place another book on top of this, and continue adding books until the paper collapses. (The paper "tower" you have made is "destroyed," hence the name "destructive" testing.) Remember how many books the paper supported, then try another paper, folded in a different way. You will probably find that one method of folding will support more books than another. By trial and error, you will finally be able to decide that one method is really stronger than all the others.

With giant presses and special molds, it is very easy for an engineer to manufacture pieces of steel in any shape he desires. These pieces of steel are called beams or girders, and many hours of thought and experimentation have produced their particular shapes. Most of them, even the biggest beams, have the same basic shapes that you have been investigating.

SPREADING YOUR WEIGHT AROUND

Suppose you weigh 100 pounds. This means that your feet must hold up 100 pounds. You have two feet. How much weight does *one* of your feet support when you are standing straight up?

This simple sounding question is actually the basis for a science principle that is very important to the engineer. *The weight of an object is divided between the supports holding it up.* This is called the distribution of weight. In your case, if you are standing straight and your weight is evenly divided between both of your feet, each foot must support just 50 pounds. Naturally, this even dividing of your weight does not always happen. If you tilt your body slightly toward the right, the right foot must hold up a greater share of the 100 pounds. But as long as you do not lift your left foot off the ground, that foot will still support · some of your weight.

It is easy to see how this rule plays an important part in the construction of buildings. The entire weight of the building will not be supported by any one steel beam or any one piece of wood. Each of the supporting beams must hold up its share of the total weight. The engineer must know what share of the weight each beam will support, and he must choose a beam strong enough to do the job properly and provide a margin of safety. You can investigate this science principle with paper beams.

A Table with Paper Legs

Things Needed:
Five sheets of paper
Sticky tape
A dozen, or more, books
(all the same size)

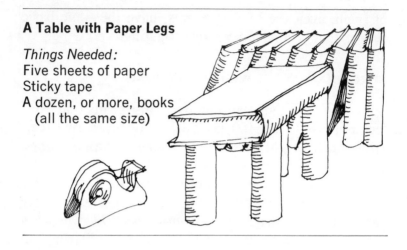

First roll the five sheets of paper into tubes. Be sure the ends of the tubes are about two inches across. All of the tubes should be the same size. (You might roll the papers around a can or bottle to be sure of this.) Fasten the edges with sticky tape so the tubes keep their shapes.

Set one tube on end on a table. Place a book on top. Balance the book carefully and, if necessary, steady it with your hand. Place another book on top of this one. Continue placing books until your tower gives way and collapses. Remember how many books one tube supported before it collapsed.

Now place the remaining four tubes on the table, like the legs on a table. Place one book on top, like a table top. How many books do you suppose this table will support? If each leg can support one-fourth of the total weight, doesn't it seem reasonable to guess that the four tubes should be able to hold four times the weight that one tube could? Continue piling books on the table—steady it with your hand until it gives way, and find out!

Suppose you piled three books on one tube, but could only pile 11 on the four tube-legged table. Would this "break the rule" of distribution of weight? Shouldn't four legs support 12 books if one leg could support three?

When you stand on two legs, each leg should support half your weight, but, if you are tipped slightly to the side, one leg might have to support more than half, right? Perhaps you did not pile your books evenly and one leg received more than one-fourth of the weight. This leg, with the extra weight, would certainly collapse first, and that would tumble the entire table.

Even in a building, one beam may have to support more weight than another. The engineer must know this and, if he cannot divide the weight more evenly, he must make that one beam a bit stronger than the others.

If this investigation intrigues you, and you would like to do some paper engineering on your own, here are some more ideas:

Can you make the table legs in another shape (other than a round tube) that will enable you to pile on more books?

Can you devise a way of piling half of the books evenly over all the legs and the other half just on the right side? This would mean that the right side must support more weight than the left.

Make a table with just one book on top, then make four more paper legs and put them on top of the book . . . another book on these legs . . . then more legs and more books . . . how high a tower can you build? Remember that each set of four legs must support all the weight above it. The bottom set must support the greatest weight. Should these legs be different shapes than the legs used in the upper part of the tower?

THE SHAPES IN BUILDING

L, T, H, I and U . . . probably these are just letters in the alphabet to you, but to the engineer, these are the very basic shapes for beams. The letters show the shape that the beam would appear if it were observed from one end. Every one of these is stronger than a beam made from a flat piece of metal, and each one would have a special job to do in a building. The engineer must carefully select the right beam for the right job. It must be the right shape to fit, and it must be strong enough to support its part of the building.

Making Model Beams

Things Needed:
Four sheets
  of typing paper
Ruler
Pencil

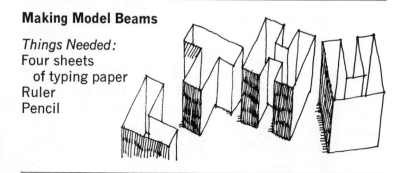

Fold each of the papers as shown in the illustration. By folding carefully, you can make I, T, U, and L beam models. You will also understand why they are named for letters in the alphabet. These beams would make an interesting classroom display. I beams are sometimes called H beams . . . can you see why? If you make the top and bottom of an I beam longer, it becomes H. The U beam is also sometimes called a box beam.

Which of these shapes is the strongest? If you want to destroy your models, you could try the destructive test on each of them to help you decide.

Why are there so many shapes? Some shapes would fit better into tight places, some are stronger than others. Some beams are specially designed to hold bricks or cement, or to have wooden beams fastened to them, and still others must be attractive shapes because people will be able to see them in the finished building. Each beam will have special jobs in the building, and their jobs will determine their shapes. If, for example, a beam will support a floor or a ceiling, it might be a very different shape from a wall beam. You'll see why in the next section.

FORCES DOWN . . . FORCES ACROSS

It should not surprise you to learn that so far in this chapter you have been investigating just *one* thing an engineer is concerned with. You have been investigating how materials behave when they are subjected to the effect of squeezing. This squeezing is called *compression*. You have discovered that paper cannot be compressed too much because it will squash easily.

However, not all the beams in a building are being squeezed. This is true of beams in the walls of buildings, but how about beams in the floors or ceilings? The beams that run across are being pushed down along their lengths. The force of being *bent* is called *flexure*. How would the paper beams you've invented so far resist being bent?

To see the difference, here is another puzzle you might like to solve:

A Paper "Bridge"

Things Needed:
Sheet of typing paper
Three plastic drinking glasses

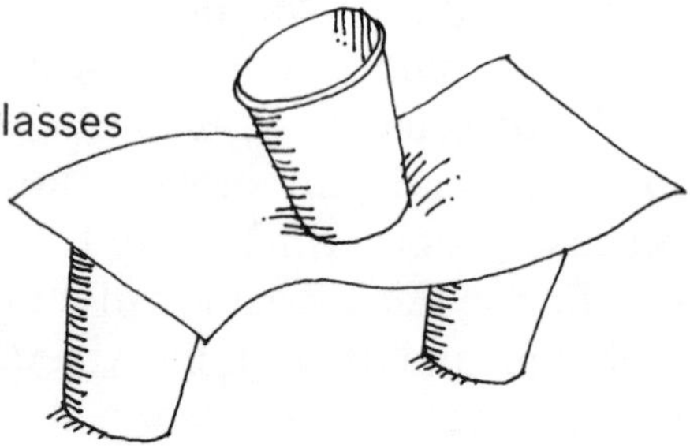

Place two plastic drinking glasses on the table with approximately six inches of space between them. Lay a sheet of paper across their tops. Set another plastic drinking glass on the bridge in the center. Will the bridge support it?

Again, the paper is much too floppy and will not support the weight of the glass. In fact, it will probably sag, unable to support its own weight. The weight of the glass is much greater, and the paper collapses.

Your challenge is to make a paper bridge out of a single sheet of paper that will support the weight of the glass. Naturally, you cannot use anything but the paper and the glasses. How can you do it?

Perhaps you already know. This puzzle has been a favorite trick of magicians for many years. Long ago people discovered that a sheet of paper could make a bridge that would support a drinking glass if it were folded back and forth in an accordion pleat several times. If you study this bridge, you will understand why it is stronger.

There are many other shapes you might use to make a paper bridge that would span two drinking glasses. You might fold the paper into a triangular shape, or a square, or a cylinder. Each of these bridges will support some weight in the center. Naturally, some of these will support more weight than others, as you found in your destructive testing investigation, but because the force is now one of flexure rather than compression, the strongest shape may not be the same as before. You will have to do still another investigation to decide which shape is the best for flexure. Here's how:

Testing Flexure with your Finger

Things Needed:
Several sheets of typing paper
Two glasses

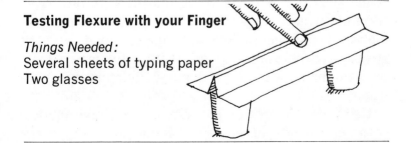

Fold, or roll, the papers into different shapes. Place each, in turn, across the two drinking glasses. Press down on the center of each bridge with your finger, until it folds and collapses. You will discover that your finger is very sensitive and you can easily decide which shape withstands the most pressure before it collapses. Which shape withstands the greatest pressure (or weight) before it folds? Is the same shape the best for both the force of compression and the force of flexure? Would an engineer be wise to select a different shape beam for a wall than for a ceiling?

BUILDING BETTER BRIDGES

One of man's biggest problems is crossing over water. We can use a boat, or perhaps we can swim across, but when we have to transport materials or cross many times, usually the easiest solution is to build a road over the water. This road is called a bridge. Bridges are designed by engineers, and the construction of paper bridges is a worthy challenge to any amateur engineer and a fine way to end this chapter.

We have already learned that a flat sheet of paper is very weak when it must bridge two drinking glasses. A flat steel bridge stretched across the span of a river certainly would not be able to support the weight of many automobiles unless an engineer made it very strong. How could he do that? Engineers have devised many ways . . . and many different kinds of bridges.

Using only pieces of paper, you can make models of several kinds of bridges. Remember that every

time you build a bridge, you must overcome the force
of flexure, or downward stress. How do these different
designs overcome this stress?

A Model Beam Bridge

Things Needed:
Piece of typing paper
Two drinking glasses
Some pennies

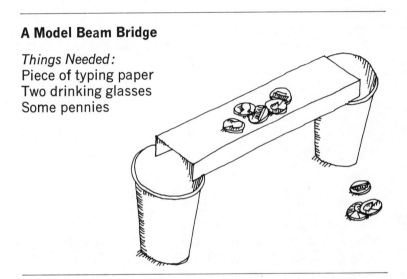

What is a beam? It is a structure that stands stiff
without any outside help, and that sounds like what
we need for a good bridge. To make a beam bridge,
cut a piece of paper eleven inches long and four inches
wide. Measure off a one inch strip on each side and
fold the edges up along these lines. (See illustration.)
Rest the ends of this beam on the drinking glasses.

Now, stack pennies on the center of the bridge until
it collapses. Remember how many pennies it supported.
Can you think of a beam bridge in your town? Many
railroad bridges are made in this shape.

Make a Model Arch Bridge

Things Needed:
Two pieces of typing paper
Two drinking glasses
Some pennies

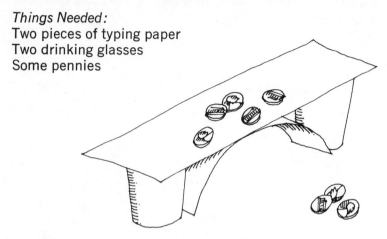

Study the illustration to make the arch bridge. Cut strips of paper three inches wide. Cut one strip the proper length to stretch across the tops of the two glasses. Cut the other the correct length to be the height of the glasses when it is arched between them. You will have to determine the correct lengths for both papers because glasses may be different sizes and different distances apart.

Again, lay pennies on top of the bridge. Will an arch bridge support more or less weight than a beam bridge? Can you see how the arch is supporting both the force of flexure and the force of compression? If you were making bridges out of steel, and large enough to span great rivers, which type of bridge do you think would be the more expensive?

Make a Model Pier Bridge

Things Needed:
Several sheets of typing paper
Sticky tape
Two drinking glasses
Some pennies

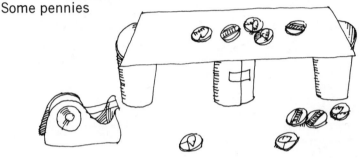

The illustration will help you to construct another type of bridge. The paper must be cut to make a roadway over the bridge, and a sheet must also be cut to the height of the drinking glasses. Form this sheet into a cylinder, and fasten it with sticky tape. This pier will be placed under the center of the roadway. Again pile pennies on the bridge. How many pennies will it support? Will it support this much weight if the coins are placed *between* the pier (or pile) and the glasses? This is the most common kind of bridge, and you have probably seen one in your area or in a book.

There are many other shapes for bridges. Perhaps you might like to investigate them, on your own, by making models of them out of paper. They are not included in this chapter because you will require other materials—string, straws, and glue—and their construction is quite a bit more complicated. Each one has been designed to be stronger, or easier to build, or less expensive.

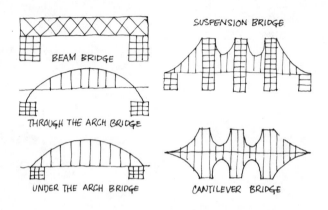

One final note on bridges: practically no two bridges look exactly alike, and yet engineers say there are only *four* different kinds of bridges built by man. These are the arch, the beam, the cantilever, and the suspension bridges.

5

Math Magic With Paper

Magicians do tricks with a great variety of objects. Those who like animals use rabbits or doves. Others use silk handkerchiefs, and still others use decks of cards. If you like science, and also enjoy fooling your friends, you would do well if you chose a piece of paper to do your magic. With just a paper, a pencil, and a little knowledge of mathematics, it is surprisingly easy to astound your friends and, best of all, to amaze even yourself.

Magicians trick us in many ways. This chapter will remind you of some of them. You can fool your friend's brain with Two Fishermen and Five Fish, and Ten Letters in Nine Envelopes. You can confuse his eye with The Wonderful Vanishing Line. You can fool him with straight arithmetic in Your Friend's Age. If you try Double Trouble or Why I Can't Go To School you may even fool yourself.

Most wonderful of all, unlike most real magic tricks, Math Magic will also teach you something. Rather than being left confused, you may just discover that you finish by knowing more than when you started.

HOW TO MAIL TEN LETTERS IN NINE ENVELOPES

If you enjoy puzzles that have a mathematical solution, here is one that seems impossible, yet you can do it, and yet, you know you can't! Can you understand why it appears to work?

"There was a boy who had ten letters to be mailed. He had only nine envelopes and, because each letter was being sent to a different address, it appeared that he was just one envelope short. But instead of searching for another envelope he did manage to fit all ten letters into the nine envelopes he had, without mailing two letters in any one envelope." Here's how:

Try This As You Read

Things Needed:
Nine small pieces of paper

Each piece of paper will represent a letter to be mailed. You will use imaginary envelopes. Start by holding all the sheets in your hand. As you read the story aloud, do the things in the parentheses.

"First, he put one letter in the first envelope." (Lay one sheet on the table.)

"For just a moment he put the second letter, with the first one, in the first envelope." (Lay another sheet on top of the one on the table.)

"He put the third letter in the second envelope." (Lay another sheet beside the first two.)

"The fourth letter went into the third envelope." (Lay another sheet beside those on the table.)

"The fifth letter went into the fourth envelope." (Lay down another sheet.)

"The sixth letter went into the fifth envelope." (Lay down another sheet.)

"The seventh letter into the sixth envelope." (Lay another sheet down.)

"The eighth letter into the seventh envelope." (Lay another sheet down.)

"The ninth letter went into the eighth envelope." (Lay down the last sheet in your hand.) "And, because this was the ninth letter, but only the eighth envelope, he could then take the tenth letter out of the first envelope (pick up one sheet from the first pile) and put this tenth letter into the ninth envelope!" (Lay the sheet at the end of the row.)

How is this possible? You may have to try it several times to convince yourself that it actually happens!

This is a mystery I would like to leave for you to solve. If you count the letters you find that you actually have only nine, which is the same number of envelopes you have. Still, you end by saying the "tenth letter goes into the ninth envelope." This is a clue to discovering how this puzzle appears to work. Is this a mathematical puzzle, or simply a puzzle with words? Even when you solve the mystery you will find that you can easily fool your friends with the same story.

THE WONDERFUL VANISHING LINE

If someone drew a line four inches long on a piece of paper and, suddenly, before your eyes, the line vanished . . . would you call it a wonderful magic trick? Actually there is a very easy way you can do this trick, and you don't have to be a magician at all. In fact, the first time you do it, it may even surprise you! Here's how:

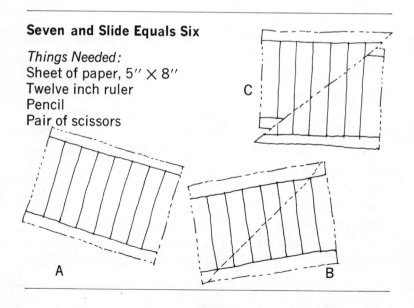

Seven and Slide Equals Six

Things Needed:
Sheet of paper, 5″ × 8″
Twelve inch ruler
Pencil
Pair of scissors

A

B

C

Draw a light line, half an inch in, along each of the eight-inch sides of the paper. Mark off these two lines at one-inch intervals. Draw heavy, straight, lines between the one-inch marks. (Figure A in the illustration will help you do this properly.)

Now, draw a single line from the bottom of the first heavy line to the top of the last one (figure B). Continue this line to the edges of the paper. Cut along this diagonal line with your scissors.

With the paper even on the ends, count the lines. You will find there are seven of them. Now, slide the bottom piece to the left, along the diagonal cut. Line up the heavy lines as shown in figure C in the illustration. Now count the lines. You will discover only six! Where did the seventh line go?

When you do this for the first time you may be startled by the sudden disappearance of the seventh line. Remember that it is not a magic trick at all, but a mathematical one. Can you figure out why this is so before reading further?

Here is an example which may help you to understand: Suppose you had seven buckets half filled with water. Your friend counts them, and agrees that you do indeed have seven buckets of water. He then turns his back, and you take one of the buckets and pour a bit of water from it into each of the remaining six buckets until all the water is gone from your bucket. Now each of the six remaining buckets contains just a bit (1/6th) more water than it contained previously. When your friend turns around he will probably not notice this, but he certainly will notice that the seventh bucket is empty. He might try to explain this by saying the water in the seventh bucket must have disappeared.

This is about the same thing that has happened with your paper. When you shifted the paper, each of the remaining six lines was a bit longer than it was at the start. If you measure the original lines with a ruler, you will find they are four inches long. After shifting the paper, each line will be about four and five-eights inches long (actually 4.6666667 inches). The extra line did not vanish after all; it was simply divided into small portions with each portion being distributed among the remaining six lines.

Human eyes are very poor at judging length. This is one reason why rulers are so necessary for measuring things. Therefore, you will probably not observe that each line is a bit longer, and it is far easier to say one line has vanished.

You can not only make a line vanish with this trick; you can also make an extra line appear. Using the same paper as before, begin with the pieces in their proper alignment, then slide the bottom piece to the right until the lines match. You will discover, if you count them, that you have eight lines, although the lines to the right and the left are much longer than those in the middle. Where did the extra line come from? It was made by stealing a little bit from each of the original seven lines. In the same way, you could make eight buckets of water by pouring a tiny bit from seven buckets into an eighth one!

If the appearance of eight lines surprises you, keep on shifting the lower paper to the right and you should be able to make nine, ten, or even twelve lines; but by then you will find the central ones growing so much shorter that the solution to the mystery becomes obvious.

DOUBLE TROUBLE

Once upon a time there was a boy who made extra money by mowing lawns. He was also, as you shall see, very clever with arithmetic. He agreed to cut a neighbor's lawn all summer long with this arrangement: "I will cut your lawn the first time for 1¢. You must pay me twice as much (2¢) the second time, double it again (4¢) for the third time, and continue to double it for each additional time." "O.K.," said his neighbor, thinking of having his lawn cut for only a few pennies.

During the summer the boy cut the lawn twenty times. "How much do I owe you?," the neighbor asked in the fall. The boy's answer left him breathless.

"You owe me $7,290.88," said the boy, and he was absolutely right! This is a make-believe story; however, if you, like the boy, are good at mathematics you will readily understand why the fee was so high. If you can't believe it, here is a simple investigation that will help you, and it won't cost you any money.

You Can't Cut This Paper In Half

Things Needed:
Piece of paper
  (any size or thickness)
Scissors

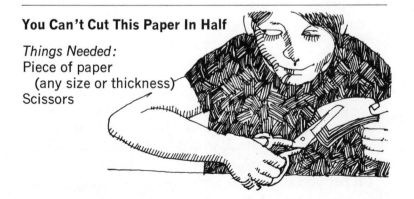

Cut the paper in half with the scissors. Lay the two pieces on top of each other and cut them in half again. Stack these pieces and cut them in half, all at the same time. Keep stacking the papers and cutting them. How many times can you continue doing this? I'll bet you can't make more than ten cuts in this way!

Why? We might call it "double trouble," but a mathematician would probably call it a *mathematical progression*. Let's see what it means. Each time you stack the papers you have exactly double the number you had before. You start with one sheet, cut it to make two, the two become four, the four become eight, and so forth. Perhaps this doesn't sound too bad, but let's see what happens after ten cuts:

0 cuts =	1	sheet of paper
1 cut =	2	sheets of paper
2 cuts =	4	sheets of paper
3 cuts =	8	sheets of paper
4 cuts =	16	sheets of paper
5 cuts =	32	sheets of paper
6 cuts =	64	sheets of paper
7 cuts =	128	sheets of paper
8 cuts =	256	sheets of paper
9 cuts =	512	sheets of paper
10 cuts =	1,024	sheets of paper

So, after ten cuts you will have 1,024 sheets stacked up to be cut for the eleventh cut. Do you think you are strong enough to cut through 1,024 sheets of paper with one snip? The stack would be several times thicker than this entire book!

I'll bet you can't fold a piece of paper in half more than nine times! You now know why you can safely make this bet with a friend. You know that after nine folds the paper will be 512 sheets thick: much too thick to fold again. What if your friend, after he had tried it once, asked if he could use a giant piece of paper—should you let him? By all means! Remember, as he doubles the thickness he is also halving the size (try it and see). If he began with a sheet of paper 100 feet long, it would only be a little more than two inches wide (and 512 pages thick) after his ninth fold. He couldn't possibly fold that stack in half! The best part of this mathematical trick is, if you don't understand it, you can easily try-it-yourself and see it happen.

FISHY MATHEMATICS

Magicians have many different ways of fooling you. They may confuse your brain, make you look the wrong way at the right time, or hide their actions behind a piece of equipment. Most people are not careful observers. Here is a math-magic trick that proves just this:

Two Fishermen and Five Fish

Things Needed:
Two cardboard boxes
Seven balls of crumpled paper
  (all the same size)

Invite a friend to watch a trick. Place the two cardboard boxes on a table and seat your friend on the floor so he cannot see inside the boxes. Place the seven paper balls on the table in front of the boxes. Arrange the balls so that two are in front of one box, and the remaining five are in front of the other. Now, here is the story you tell him:

"Once there were two fishermen. (Pick up the two paper balls.) One morning they both went fishing, each in his own boat. (Place one ball in each box.) After a while, one of them caught a fish. (Place one of the five balls in one of the boxes.) Then the other fisherman caught a fish. (Place a ball in the other box.) All through the morning one would catch a fish, then the other." (Place the third ball in the first box, the fourth, in the second, and the fifth in the first box.)

"Just then, one of the fishermen heard a motorboat. He remembered that he had forgotten his fishing license and was afraid the fishing warden might be coming in the motorboat. He decided to throw back the fish. (Throw one ball from the second box back on the table.) The first fisherman remembered that he had forgotten his fishing license too, so he decided to return his fish to the water, also. (Throw one ball from the first box onto the table.) The other fisherman threw a fish back. (Return another ball from the second box to the table.) The first fisherman did the same (return a ball from the first box to the table), and the other fisherman threw the last fish back. (Return a ball from the second box to the table.) Now the five fish were back in the pond."

"As soon as they had returned all the fish, the motor-boat noise stopped, and the fishermen began fishing once again. It wasn't long before the first fisherman caught another fish. (Drop one ball from the table into the first box.) Then the second fisherman caught one. (Drop a ball from the table into the second box.) Then the first (drop a ball from the table into the first box), then the second (drop a ball from the table into the second box), then the first (drop a ball from the table into the first box), and so forth until five fish were back in the boats." (Drop the remaining two balls in the first and second boxes.)

"Just then, the motorboat returned, and this time it was the fish warden. He came right up to the boats and took a long look. What do you think he saw? Not a fisherman in each boat with some fish: No! In one boat he found the two fishermen (dump the two balls out of the second box), and in the other boat, all by themselves, were the five fish (dump out the five balls in the first box)!"

Do not look for a magic trick here. No sleight of hand is required. This is not magic, it is simple mathematics. It depends on just two things: the paper balls representing the fish and the fishermen look just the same, and there are an even number of fishermen and boats but there are an odd number of fish.

The surprise is that you finish with two balls in one box and five in the other, although it appears that you divided them equally between both boxes. Let's look at a diagram and you will readily understand how this happens:

At the start you place two fishermen (balls) into two boats (boxes), and leave five fish on the table.

One "fish" is placed in the first box.

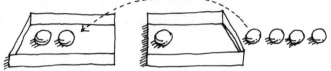

The next fish goes into the second box;

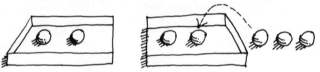

the third into the first box;

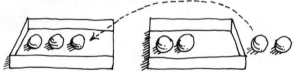

the fourth into the second box;

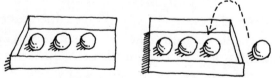

the last fish goes into the first box;

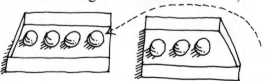

Now here is the math-magic of the trick. When the fishermen hear the motorboat the first fish to be returned is *from the second box:*

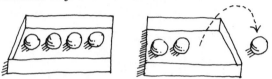

The next comes from the first box;

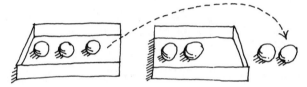

the next from the second box;

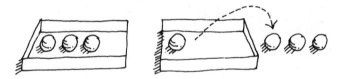

another from the first box;

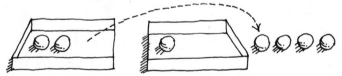

and another from the second box.

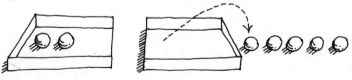

Now, again a bit of math-magic: the motorboat noise goes away and the two fishermen start fishing once again. *The first to catch a fish is the man in the first boat.*

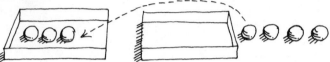

Then the other catches a fish.

Then the first catches another fish;

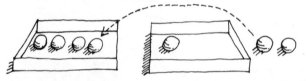

then the second;

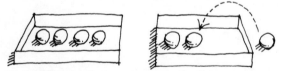

then the first fisherman catches the last fish.

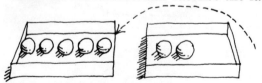

Because the fish and the fishermen look the same, it is now easy to say that the two balls in the second boat are the two fishermen, and the five balls in the first boat are the five fish.

You can readily understand how this happens if you actually try the trick, or study the illustrations; but, if you try it with a friend you will find he is puzzled by this math trick. He will not remember exactly what you did, or in what order you did it. He may credit you with some sleight of hand which, of course, you did not use. If, by chance, your friend does understand how you did it, you certainly should compliment him on having an extraordinary sense of observation.

YOUR FRIEND'S AGE

Paper was made for writing on. Some of the very best math-magic tricks can be done with a piece of paper and pencil. For example, have you ever wondered how old a friend was? With paper, pencil, and some interesting arithmetic you can not only find out how old he is, but the month, and the day of the month, he was born on. All your friend must do is honestly answer some simple questions.

Telling Your Friend's Age

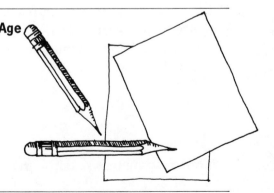

Things Needed:
Two sheets of paper
Two pencils

Give your friend one of the sheets of paper and a pencil. Ask him to write down the following things, and do the following arithmetic:

1. The date and month of his birth. If he was born on the twelfth of May he would first write down 12 for the day, then 5 for the month. (May is the fifth month.) His figure would read 125.
2. Tell him to multiply this number by two. (In this case, 2 × 125 is 250.)
3. Ask him to add five to this figure. (This makes 255 in our example.)
4. He must then multiply this figure by 50. (255 × 50 is 12750 in our example.)
5. Now ask him to add his present age to this figure. (Let's say your friend is 12. Then 12750 + 12 = 12762.)
6. And, finally, he should add the number of days in a year, 365. (In our example, 12762 + 365 gives 13127.)
7. Ask him to give you just this final figure.

In our example, you would receive the number 13127. To determine your friend's age and birthday you need only write down this figure on your paper and subtract the magic number 615 from it. This new figure will give you all of the information you require.

```
  13127
−   615
  12512
```

Your new figure, 12512, is read from the left. The first figures give you the day: it is the twelfth. The

next figure gives the month, 5: the fifth month is
May. The last two figures tell you that your friend is
12 years old.

This is an easy trick to do, and it will work for any
friend you might have, regardless of his birthday.
But why does it always work?

To understand this you must study the steps your
friend takes very carefully. Notice that the second
step is to multiply by two, and step number four is to
multiply by 50. This is the same as asking him to
multiply by 100. ($2 \times 50 = 100$) So, in effect, you
are simply asking your friend to multiply his original
number by 100 . . . which is the same as asking him
to just add two zeros to his original number. You have,
however, done two things to confuse him:

First you made it a two step multiplication to disguise
the fact that all you really had him do was multiply
by 100.

Second, in step number three you asked him to add
five. However, regardless of his original number you
will only increase the total by 250 after the fourth
step is completed. ($50 \times 5 = 250$). This allows you
to keep track of his original number. You know that
his original number has been multiplied by 100, and
that 250 has been added to it. Hence, you have not
lost his original number; you still know just how to
find it!

In the fifth step you ask him to add his age. This is
necessary because it is some information that you
want to know. Now all you have is: his original number
multiplied by 100, plus 250, plus his age. Now, all
you have to do is eliminate all of the unnecessary

numbers you have given him, and add enough confusion to prevent him from catching on.

In step number six he adds 365, the number of days in a year. This is just to distract your friend from the important arithmetic. It makes the final total larger, and less likely to be suspicious to your friend.

To solve the problem, you simply subtract 615 from his total. This is not a made-up number. It is the total made of 365 (step number 6 and 250 from steps 3 and 4). $365 + 250 = 615$, and 615 subtracted from the total your friend gives you will leave you only the numbers you really want, the date, month, and age!

If you can understand how and why you were able to quickly find your friend's age and birthday by remembering the extra steps you took and eliminating these, you might like to try a similar trick on yourself:

Write down *any* number you like
Multiply this number by 4
Add 5 to the new total
Multiply the new total by 25

Now, subtract 125 from the final total and I'll bet the *left hand* number(s) of this number is the original number(s) you wrote down! Now, can you explain why this works?

WHY I CAN'T GO TO SCHOOL

Here is a final math-magic trick you might like to try ... but it probably won't work for you! If you don't like to go to school, maybe you can explain to your parents that you just "don't have the time."

School Daze

Things Needed:
Paper
Pencil
Parent

Using a paper and pencil, try this "I just don't have time to go to school" lecture on your mother or father:

"There are only 365 days in the year."
(Write 365 on the paper.)
"If I sleep 10 hours a day, this amounts to 152 days every year."

(Write:)   365
     − 152
     213 days left in the year

"There is no school on weekends, and there are 104 Saturdays and Sundays in a year."

(Write:)   213
     − 104
     109 days left in the year

"Summer vacation lasts two months. This means I can't go to school 60 days a year!"

(Write:)   109
     − 60
     49 days left in the year

"I need at least 3 hours a day for eating and playing. This amounts to about 45 days a year."

(Write:)   49
          -45
         $\overline{4}$ days left in the year

"This leaves only 4 days a year for school and, with at least 4 school holidays during the year, that really leaves me with zero days left to go to school!"

Naturally there must be something wrong with this kind of figuring. Can you see what it is? If you can't, I'll bet your mom or dad can! (Here's a final hint: do you eat and sleep on your summer vacation?)

6

Final Fun-damentals

If so far in our science safari you have learned one or two things that you did not know when you started, you can consider your expedition a success! But the safari is not yet over. There are still many things you can explore with science and paper. This final chapter contains many more adventures and ideas. You will investigate with fire, water, snow, and scissors. And some of the mysteries will leave you something to think about after you put this book back on the shelf.

START THINKING

Here's an idea to start your brain thinking for itself. Suppose you wanted to write a secret message to a friend. How could you do it? Here are two ways.

Take a page of newspaper; be sure that it has words on it, and not pictures. Suppose your secret message was to be "Come and see me soon." How could you use the paper to send it? Just push a pin through each

Punching Paper

Things Needed:
Sheet of newspaper
A pin

> **Newspaper**
>
> Can you make any sense out of this secret code? See the message in this investigation on following pages.

letter—COME—as you come to it in the newspaper sheet. Continue punching until you have spelled out all of your message. Send this punched paper to your friend. Now, all he has to do is hold it up to the light and write down the punched letters in their correct order. This will spell out your message.

How else could you do it? Perhaps you could use a plain sheet of writing paper and write your message on it in invisible ink. Just write on a piece of paper with any of the liquids listed in the Invisible Writing investigation.

Invisible Writing

Things Needed:
Lemon juice
Onion juice
Pen, or small brush
A little sugar in water
Milk

Once these "inks" are dry, all your friend has to do is hold the paper over a warm oven (or a hot light bulb) for a few moments and your invisible writing will appear.

Both of these methods of secret writing have been used by spies for many years. A good scientist could easily think of still other methods. Can you?

NOTHING'S THE SAME

You have probably heard that no two people in the world have exactly the same fingerprints. Do you also know that no two of anything in the world are exactly the same?

Pick a leaf from a tree . . . any kind of tree. I'll bet you can't find another leaf on that tree, or any tree of the same kind, that matches your leaf exactly.

Choose two of your mother's glasses which look identical. Are they really twins? They probably look alike, but I'll bet one is a little different from the other.

Tap the side of one to make it ring like a bell. Then tap the other one. They will probably make a slightly different sound.

Have you ever seen anyone who looks just like you? Have you ever seen a school that looks just like yours? Have you ever seen two rocks which are exactly alike? It is one of the most amazing and wondrous facts that no two of anything you can see are absolutely just the same. But most people have a hard time believing this fact. To investigate, let us select one part of a person to check, the *fingerprints*.

Pencil and Paper Prints

Things Needed:
Two pieces of white paper
Sticky, transparent tape
A pencil

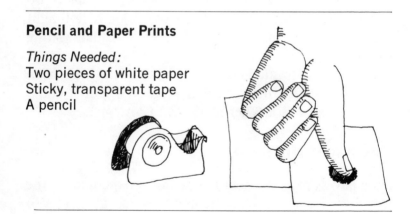

Take one sheet of paper and rub the side of the pencil point on it until you have a black smudge about an inch wide. Rub your thumb hard in this smudge. As you rub your thumb in the smudge, roll your thumb from side to side to be certain that all parts of the end of your thumb are covered with pencil lead. When you have a nice layer of lead on your thumb, remove a piece of sticky tape, about two inches long, from the roll. Press this tape against your thumb, sticky side against the thumb. Continue pressing the tape until it sticks to all parts of your thumbprint. Now, peel off the tape. You will discover that the pencil lead sticks to the tape and peels off with it. You will see a nice thumbprint on the tape.

To preserve your print, simply stick the tape down on the clean sheet of paper. You will be able to see the print clearly but, because it is covered by the tape, it can't smudge. Label this print, "My right (left) thumb." You might wish to make similar prints of all your other fingers.

Next, try printing your family and your friends. Compare the prints. Are you all the same? Can you find the differences?

If you become interested in fingerprints, the next step might be to *classify* the different prints in your collection according to the patterns they make. You don't have to do this by yourself; it has already been done for you by the Federal Bureau of Investigation (the FBI) of the United States Department of Justice. Here are some types you might look for:

Tented Arch   Plain Arch   Plain Whorl

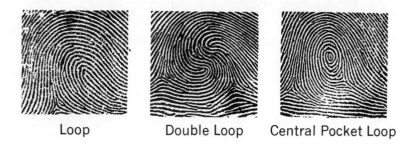

Loop   Double Loop   Central Pocket Loop

With a little library research, or perhaps a visit to your local police office, you can learn other, more complicated, differences in fingerprints.

Does anyone in the world have exactly the same fingerprints as you? The answer now might surprise you. Yes, there is a chance that someone has. Why? There are only so many patterns that fingerprints can take, and there are many millions of people in the world. A mathematician would tell you that there is a chance that two people might have the same patterns in their fingerprints. Does this mean that the two of you are exactly the same? Don't you suppose the person with the same fingerprints as you might have hair or eyes of a different color than yours? Perhaps he is taller or heavier than you. Maybe his arms are longer or his toes are shorter. Is there anyone in the world just exactly like you?

PAPER—HOT AND COLD

Benjamin Franklin was one of America's great men. He was a philosopher, a politician, and a scientist.

You might be saying to yourself, "Yes, he flew a kite during a thunderstorm and discovered that lightning is electricity." But this was only one of Franklin's many science experiments. Benjamin Franklin was an experimenter—an investigator—just like you. Science was his hobby and, during his life, he investigated many things and wrote about them.

Way back in the year 1761, Franklin performed an investigation dealing with bits of cloth, snow, and the sun. You can try the same thing with paper, if you live in a place where there is snow.

Papers on the Snow

Things Needed:
A piece of black paper
A piece of white paper
A yard covered with snow
A sunny day

The experiment Franklin did was simply to lay pieces of cloth on the snow and leave them for the day. You could do the same, using your papers in place of cloth; they work the same way. If the day is windy, place a small rock, or weight of some kind on each of the papers so they won't blow away. Use identical weights to make sure conditions are the same for both pieces of paper. You must start the investigation in the morning and leave it in place until late afternoon.

When Franklin returned to his experiment he discovered an interesting fact: the white paper was still on top of the snow but the black paper had sunk down into it.

Why did this happen? Surprisingly, the magic word is neither paper, snow, black, white, nor sun; the magic word is *heat*. The heat, of course, comes from the sun. When this heat strikes the earth, one of two things can happen to it: it may *reflect* off what it hits, or it may be *absorbed* by the object. Why doesn't the snow melt when the hot sunlight hits it? Does the white snow reflect or absorb the heat?

White or light-colored objects act like heat mirrors and do not absorb much of the sun's heat. Just the opposite is true of black or dark-colored objects. These absorb the sun's heat and become warmer. This was what Franklin proved in 1761, and this is what you are also proving.

If you are smart, you will dress in light-colored clothing in the hot days of summer, and in dark-colored clothing during the cold days of winter. Your clothes, like the papers, will absorb or reflect heat depending on what color they are.

Space ships are usually painted white, or some light color. Do you think now that it is just to make them beautiful? Some early rockets were painted with black and white stripes. Can you understand how this helped them to keep an even temperature inside, even though they were high above the earth where the sunlight was even hotter?

It is easy to see, with these examples and others you might think of yourself, that this simple rule is a very important one to us all. It is another proof that people who claim they are not interested in science are affected by it every single day of their lives.

Suppose you live where there is no snow, or perhaps it is summertime when you are reading this book. Can you do this same experiment? There is nothing about winter which makes this investigation work! The rule is true at all times during the year. All you need are the papers and some "indicator" of temperature. An ice cube will do nicely!

So There's No Snow . . .

Things Needed:
Piece of white paper
Piece of black paper
Two ice cubes of the same size

Lay the papers out flat on the ground so that the sun is shining on them. Be sure they are in a place where the sun will shine on them for at least a half hour. Put one ice cube in the center of each piece. If the cube slips to the side, hold it in place with a few pebbles around the outside. Observe both cubes as they melt. This will not take long. Which ice cube will melt first? If the one on the black paper does, you have again proven that dark colors absorb heat and get warmer faster than the light ones.

A PAPER POT

Suppose you were lost in the woods and had no pots or pans with you, and for your supper you found that you had to boil some water; how would you do it? Would it surprise you if I suggested that you make a pot out of paper?

You will probably say, "But where would I find paper in the woods?" This is easy if you remember that paper is made of plant fibres and the woods are full of those. You might use some of "nature's paper," the same kind that the American Indians used. Birch bark, or the thin bark of many trees, would serve nicely.

Now that you've found your paper, all you must do is fold it into the shape of an open-top box, pour in the water, and hold it over a fire until it boils.

But wait a minute. You are probably saying, "But paper or bark will burn if I put a fire near it." Before you worry about that, remember that this is a science book, not a book telling you how to survive in the woods if you are lost. Truthfully, the science to be investigated is just this: why doesn't the bark burn?

Before you investigate the reason why, perhaps you might like to prove to yourself that this trick really will work. You don't need bark, and you don't have to be lost in the woods. This investigation will work well with some typing paper, a frying pan, and your mother's stove. (For safety's sake an adult should be present.)

A Hot Investigation

Things Needed:
Piece of typing paper, 3″ × 3″
A frying pan
A stove
Water
Paper clips

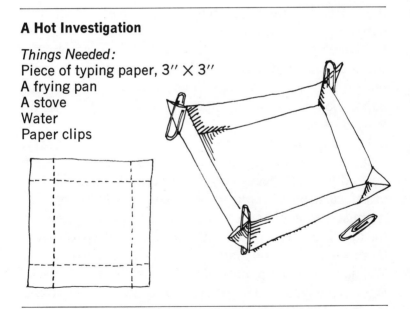

First, fold the paper into a box by folding over half an inch on each side, holding the corners in place with paper clips or a little sticky tape. (See illustration.)

Fill this box about one-third full of water. If the box leaks, the paper is not waterproof, and you will have to try another kind of paper. (A piece of slick cardboard will usually work well.) Once you have found a paper pot that does not leak, place the water-filled box in the frying pan. Place the frying pan on the burner of your mother's stove. With her permission, turn the stove on and watch the water.

There is an old expression that says, "A watched pot never boils," but this will not be true in your investigation. In a very few minutes you will discover the water beginning to bubble and boil. Once this happens, turn the heat off. As long as there is water in the paper pot, the paper will not burn or scorch, but the small amount of water will quickly boil away and, once it is gone, the paper will char. Now why does this paper box work so nicely? Why doesn't it burn? Why does anything burn?

For anything to burn three things are necessary. First, a fire must have a fuel, something that can burn. Secondly, a fire needs oxygen, or air. Lastly, the fuel must reach its *kindling temperature*, which means that it must become hot enough to join with oxygen in the air. If any one of these three necessities are missing, there can be no fire. Now let's look at the paper pot. We have fuel for a fire. The fuel is the paper itself. We have oxygen. The oxygen is in the air all around the paper pot. We seem to have the temperature because the paper is on the hot stove or fire, but here is the reason it does not burn.

If the paper gets hot enough it will reach its *kindling temperature* and will start to burn. To boil, the water in the pot must also get very hot. The water requires so much heat to boil that most of the heat from the stove passes right through the paper and raises the temperature of the water. This means that the water reaches its boiling point but the paper cannot reach its kindling temperature. Without the water, the paper would become hotter and hotter, and it would finally reach the temperature required to join with the oxygen in the air. Once this happened the paper would burst into flames.

Why not put the paper pot right on the stove? Why do you put it in the frying pan? You could put it right on the stove, but only if you folded it very carefully. To be protected from the heat, every part of the paper touching the burner must have some water next to it. If you fold the paper unevenly, so that the corners are dry, the corners will be able to reach their kindling temperature and they will quickly catch fire and burn.

The frying pan spreads the heat evenly over the bottom of the paper. Perhaps you can devise a better way of making a paper pot so that all parts of the paper will be covered on the inside with water. When you have done this, you might try this investigation without the frying pan.

Now that you know the three things needed to have a fire, you might like to try an investigation that seems a bit surprising. Paper can be used to make fires, but it can also be used to put them out. Before you read further, you might like to try to think of a way that a piece of burning paper could be extinguished with a piece of the same kind of paper.

A Paper Extinguisher for a Paper Fire

Things Needed:
Piece of typing paper
Small juice glass
Matches

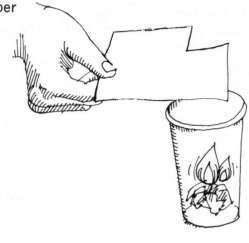

Tear a 2″ × 2″ square out of one corner of the sheet of paper. Crumple this small square into a ball. Set this on fire and quickly drop it into the glass. This will be your fire. Now, how can you put it out? There are many ways you might think of. You could blow it out; you could pour water on it; you could wait until it all burned up. The way you might try, however, is the most surprising of all; you might try laying the rest of the sheet of paper over the top of the glass! At first you will probably think this is a silly idea, because the flames might set it on fire too, but if you are careful to cover the whole top, so that there is no space between the paper and the glass, the flame will simply grow smaller and finally go out entirely.

Why does the flame go out instead of lighting the paper on top? Remember the three things required for a fire: fuel, oxygen, and heat. As long as the top of the glass was open there was plenty of each of them, but once you covered the top, the only oxygen present was in the air trapped inside the glass. The fire quickly uses that little bit of oxygen and, without it, there can be no fire. Once any one of the three necessities is missing, the fire goes out. Here are three fires that can be put out by removing one of these three necessities:

A *burning gas stove* (Shut off the gas. This eliminates the *fuel*.)

A *burning pan of grease on the stove* (Put a cover on the pan. This eliminates the *oxygen*.)

A *house on fire* (Spray water on it. This lowers the *temperature*.)

Can you think of other kinds of fires and how you would put them out? In each example you think of, try to decide which of the three necessities you are eliminating.

A ONE-SIDED PUZZLE

Probably every piece of paper you have ever seen has two sides, just like the page in this book you are reading now. Do you know that it is possible to make a piece of paper with only one side? If you don't, you might like to think about this a moment before you read further.

Because every piece of paper has two sides, it is necessary to take your pencil off one side and flip the paper over to write on the other side. If a paper had only one side, you could write on all parts of it without ever lifting your pencil off or doing any flipping. If an insect were to walk on a one-sided paper, he could walk on every part of it without ever turning any sharp corners, right? And he could always return back to where he started from. Is a paper like this possible?

A real one-sided piece of paper was discovered by a German astronomer and mathematician named Augustus Ferdinand Moebius. In his honor this one-sided paper is called the *Moebius Strip*. Moebius experimented in a kind of mathematics called *topology*, which is the study of the surfaces of objects. *Topologists*, as mathematicians who study topology are called, investigate what happens to things when they are pulled and stretched out of shape without breaking or making holes in them. Let me give you an example or two.

In my mind I could pull and stretch a nickel and make it into the shape of a piece of chewing gum, couldn't I? (Of course, in topology, we have to use our imaginations. Many of these things we really couldn't do.) Now, could I take a pair of scissors and stretch them into the shape of a piece of gum? No! Scissors would not work because they have holes in the handles. No matter how much I imagined changing their shape, the holes would always be there. To a topologist, all things without holes are the same, and all things with the same number of holes are the same. This is a very difficult idea to think about, but if you can even begin to understand it, you might make a good topologist. These examples require a very good imagination and this is only the very beginning of the study of topology.

The important idea is that topologists study the surface of things. To a topologist, a piece of paper has two sides. (He might even say it has six sides if he thinks about the edges.) If he wanted a paper with only one side, he would think about how both surfaces might be connected to make only one. That is exactly what Moebius did, and here is how he solved it.

The Famous Moebius Strip

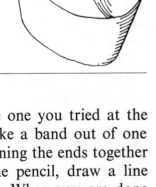

Things Needed:
Strips of newspaper two inches wide
   and the width of the
   newspaper long
Scissors
Pencil
Sticky tape

This investigation is the same one you tried at the end of Chapter One. First, make a band out of one of the strips of newspaper by joining the ends together with the sticky tape. Using the pencil, draw a line around the middle of the strip. When you are done you will discover that you have a line around one side, the outside of the strip. This piece of paper, although it is now a band, still has two sides!

Fasten the other strip of paper in a band but, before you stick the ends together, give the paper strip *one-half a twist*. Draw around the middle of this strip. You will arrive back to where you started and your line will cover all sides! Yet, you never took your pencil off the paper to "draw on the other side". This paper strip (with one twist) is the famous Moebius Strip, a piece of paper that has only one side!

Once you have made a Moebius Strip you might wish to investigate it a bit further. Naturally a piece of paper with only one side must be very different from any other piece of paper which you have ever met in your life. How different is it?

With the scissors, cut along the line you made on the first (untwisted) strip. You will finish with two separate bands of paper. This is what you can expect from a two-sided piece of paper.

Do the same cutting with the Moebius Strip (twisted band). This time you will end up with *one band* that is *twice as long*. Truly, this one-sided paper is very different.

If you wonder what happens to the other side or why the strip is twice as long, I'm afraid your questions will have to wait. Although topology is a most fascinating subject, to really understand it requires a great deal of knowledge. Perhaps this simple investigation will interest you in this "strange world of topology" and give you a special interest in it if you meet it later in your schooling.

Before you leave the Moebius Strip, you might like to try a few other investigations. Make other bands and twist them as follows.

Give one band a full twist
Give one band a twist and a half.
Cut each one of these lengthwise with your scissors. You will be surprised at the results! Now, can you think of other paper-cutting experiments you might try? Some magicians use tricks like these to fool their audiences. You can amaze your friends with them, too!

POSSIBLE IMPOSSIBILITIES

In Chapter One of this book you were introduced to Paper Impossibilities which were things you *can't* do with paper. It is only fair to end the book with a collection of "impossible" things you *can* do with paper.
  "Impossible things" are often nothing more than puzzles. When you know how to solve the puzzles, they are simple. Perhaps a few simple puzzles will show you how impossible things are easy, once you know the answers.

The Quarter Through the Hole

Things Needed:
Piece of paper
A quarter
A dime
Scissors
A pencil

Lay the dime on the sheet of paper. Draw around the dime with the pencil. Cut out the dime-size hole with scissors. Your problem now is to push the quarter through that dime-size hole. Can you do it? Try a few times before you read further.

This is not impossible. Here's how to do it. Fold the paper in half so that the crease goes through the middle of the hole. Drop the quarter between the folds and hold it through the hole with your thumb and fingers. Gently pull the quarter and it will slip through easily.

Why does it work? Fold the paper in half and hold the edge of the hole in each hand. Gently pull the two edges apart. Doesn't the hole get longer? Think of an elastic band ... when it is round the hole in the middle is a certain size, but if you flatten the band the hole gets narrow, but longer. The hole in your paper gets longer for the same reason.

Here is another hole puzzle that seems impossible when you read about it. Again, think about how it might be done before you read the solution.

Your Head Through a Hole

Things Needed:
Piece of paper, 3" × 5"
Scissors

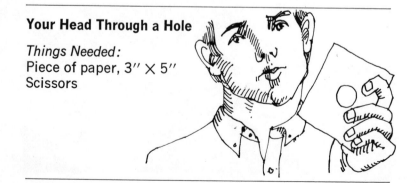

The problem? It's easy to say, but seems impossible to do. Cut a hole in the paper that is big enough to poke your head through.

Here is an easier problem that might lead you to the correct solution. Can you cut a 3″ × 5″ card into a strip of paper that is three feet long? You could do it this way:

If you could cut the card into a three-foot long strip ... then fasten the ends together ... it could make a "hole" in the middle large enough for you to put your head through, couldn't it? Can you figure out how to do just this? If not, cut your card this way:

Often impossible things only seem that way. With a little thought and ingenuity, we can usually find a solution. To finish, here are six things which might seem impossible to you when you first read them, yet every one is easily solved if you consider them carefully. Not one of them is at all "impossible."

- Can you measure with a ruler how thick one page of this book is? (Try measuring how thick all the pages are.)

- Put a sheet of newspaper on the floor in such a way that you can stand on one end and a friend can stand on the other end, and yet you will not be able to touch one another. (Here's a hint: what could you put between you and your friend?)

- If a near-sighted person, wearing glasses, were lost in the woods and had nothing but a piece of paper in his pocket, how could he start a fire to keep himself warm?

- I have an old telephone directory that I would like to tear in half. The book is much too thick and I am not strong enough to rip through all those pages. How can I tear it into two equal parts, with one rip, without using anything but my hands?

- If you had a square piece of paper with each side six inches long, could you draw a single straight line on the paper eight inches long? (If you can't imagine how, try it with a real piece of paper.)

- How would you find the exact center of a piece of paper if you couldn't use a ruler or a pencil?

Now you have reached the end of this book, but you have not yet reached the end of your science safari. Anyone who has an interest in science and the world around him will find questions to be answered, puzzles to be solved, and wonderful things to think about wherever he goes or whatever he does. Perhaps this book should be considered just a first step on your safari. You have taken a long look at paper and think of how much you have learned. Imagine how much more you can learn if you look just as hard at all the other things making up your world!

Index

ABOUT THE AUTHOR

Besides being a master builder of paper architecture, Laurence B. White, Jr. is also a member of the Society of American Magicians. Both activities may seem unrelated, but they really reflect different facets of his principle interest: the dramatic presentation of scientific ideas. As Assistant Director of the Needham (Massachusetts) Elementary Science Center and as a popular television teacher, Mr. White has had ample opportunities to use his unique talents.